When We Were Young

Two Entangled Lives

Bob McCluskey
with Agnes Mary Martin

Printed in Canada

ISBN: 978-1-4866-1286-4

Word Alive Press
131 Cordite Road, Winnipeg, MB R3W 1S1
www.wordalivepress.ca

WORD ALIVE
—P R E S S—

RECYCLED
Paper made from
recycled material
FSC® C103567

Library and Archives Canada Cataloguing in Publication

McCluskey, Bob, 1926-, author
     When we were young : two entangled lives / Bob McCluskey with Agnes
Mary Martin.

Issued in print and electronic formats.
ISBN   978-1-4866-1286-4   (paperback).--ISBN   978-1-4866-1287-1
(pdf).--
ISBN 978-1-4866-1288-8 (html).--ISBN 978-1-4866-1289-5 (epub)

     1. McCluskey, Bob, 1926-. 2. Martin, Agnes Mary, 1925-. 3.
Christian
biography. 4. Christian life. 5. God (Christianity)--Love. I. Martin,
Agnes
Mary, 1925-, author II. Title.

BR1700.3.M35 2016   248.8'5   C2016-900576-3
                                            C2016-900577-1

table of contents

Bob McCluskey on forlorn,
rainy Sunday in Toronto
in 1934, age 8

Chapter One

COME WITH ME ON A JOURNEY INTO MY FRIEND BOB'S distant, chequered past, into a time of innocence and opportunity. On the cold morning of January 18, 1926, our omnipotent Creator saw fit to unceremoniously deposit this persistent, demanding bundle into the snowy borough of East York, a suburb of Toronto, Canada. I say unceremoniously, for in those tough times I don't suppose his folks were too happy to have another mouth to feed, even though breast milk came free of charge.

Accompany me next to the borough of Smethwick, a suburb close to the grubby industrial city of Birmingham, England, where one year earlier—almost to the day, on January 20, 1925—a pink, squalling, impatient baby girl made her entrance: Agnes Mary Edmonds.

A question some might ask, and which I've wondered myself, is why He who makes these decisions, purposed to grace England with lovely baby Agnes Mary, and conversely to burden Canada with baby Bob. After all, Canada was much younger and was in sore need of as much added beauty as it could get, but let's just leave that one alone.

Bob's childhood proceeded not unlike many thousands of other children in Toronto in those pre-World War II years. A sister came along two years later, and a younger brother two years after her arrival. The Great Depression was in full swing and Bob's dad suffered much shorter working hours as a printer. They were planning to buy a small bungalow on Mortimer Avenue, but when the depression stole their home they moved a few blocks north to a rented house on Gowan Avenue. There was a great empty field a few doors down where Bob and a few newfound friends would play for hours on hot summer days.

Let Bob's dog Eugene introduce the gang: "Okay all you guys out there, now hear this! I am a dog, see, and I don't want to hear any laughing from any of you either. I can bite, you know, but I really wouldn't. I'm a pretty good dog, as dogs go. But the point is, I can write too. Oh, not the way you do, but I have a secret talent and I'm going to tell you Bobby's next story, and it's really a beaut! Bobby said it's okay to tell, even though he gets in trouble again in this story. So here we go.

"Woke up this morning to hear the door slam. My

master, Bob's dad, is off to work on the tram. Next thing, Bobby's mom flip-flops down the stairs. Dogs don't miss a thing and we're always prepared. And that's why people keep us around, I guess. We try really hard to avoid the dog pound.

"So now that it's safe, I run up the stairs and wake up sleepy Bobby. Let's go and have fun. So outside Bobby saunters, with me close behind. He looks around for the gang. They're not hard to find. There's Charlie McWhorter and his friend Tom Lesage, and there's three or four more playing mumblety-peg. As they drift together, one kicking a can, I bark the alarm.

"Sticky Pants runs up. Most of Bobby's new friends have nicknames—and all have a story attached. Here is Sticky Pants' story. His real name is Charlie Jones, and boy is he a character. Charlie hates mashed potatoes, and at dinner, when no one is looking, he stuffs handfuls of mashed potatoes in his pockets. If I'm there, he puts his messy hand down for me to lick it clean, which is fine with me; dogs love mashed potatoes. I love to sit under his table, where lots of good food comes down. I clean up his mess and help keep him from trouble, I guess, for acting the clown.

"Well, one day when his mom was doing the laundry, she noticed Charlie's pen knife. She put her hand in his pocket to take it out, and boy did she let out a yell. She cried, 'Charlie's pants are so sticky!' The whole neighbourhood heard it, and from then on they called Charlie 'Sticky Pants.'

"But I wander away from my story, and I'll tell you, it's really a beaut. Here come three ladies. They pet me and say I'm real cute. But the boys help me run for cover. There's a field down the street where we can hide. There, Sticky Pants shares his secret. He's really busting with pride. He's found these plans for an underground fort, and they can 'borrow' all the tools they'll need from home.

"Well, digging an underground fort is pretty serious stuff, so the gang decides they'd better hold a secret meeting in their secret hiding place. They fly up Pape Avenue to their secret cave in the brush, all looking quite grim. To secrecy swear, or they'll cut off his hair, with a knife, from his chinny-chin-chin. Though I'm in the gang, I'm safe from the knife; I'm a doggy, and they know I can't squeal. But I wouldn't betray, 'cause I can't anyway. Dogs stay faithful, however they feel.

"But let me get back to my 'tail,' and please, don't interrupt again because I'm bound by the doggy creed to always tell the truth. Bet you didn't know that, eh? And something else I bet you don't know: dogs can count. Listen… Dad, Mom, and Bobby makes three. Pretty smart, eh?

"So we all scoot out of our hideout and fly back to our homes, me in front 'cause I'm the fastest. The gang is pretty excited about digging that underground fort and want to get started right away. They each go into their basements to scrounge for shovels and boxes to carry all the dirt away from the hole.

"Sticky Pants is posted out on the street as lookout and I stand guard with him. Then, when the coast is clear, he gives them the signal and they all scoot over to the vacant field and look for just the right spot to dig their fort, trying to act very casual and innocent. Carrot Top is elected to mark out the fort on the ground, because his dad is a builder. They make him wear a cap to hide his flaming red hair, but he can't hide his flaming red freckles. His real name's Freddy Gilbert.

"Now that digging time is upon them, they must allocate all the work. Tom Lesage is in charge of the shovels, if he promises to take off that cape. Fat Mickey Flynn—they all call him Slim—becomes breathless when working too long. So their guard he will be, watching for danger with me, his bird whistle blowing a song.

"So they all start digging but there are too many people and they're getting in each other's way. So some of the guys are put in charge of saving and piling the sod, and others carry boxes of dirt and spread it away from the fort. A couple of the gang is put in charge of gathering lots of strong branches to use for a roof. If Slim blows his bird whistle, we'll all hit the deck and wait 'til danger passes. A couple of older ladies are pretty curious.

"When the hole is as deep as we need, and the walls are cut just right, strong branches are placed over the top. Now the fort is out o' sight. The next layer they pave, all the sod that they save, now is blended right in with the field. With box chairs and tables and candles and cups, they'll meet there, fully concealed.

"Well, I wish this was the end of my story, but there's a little more I must tell. We enjoyed our fort clubhouse for a few days. But then, suddenly, when no one was in the fort, something happened that the boys hadn't thought about. The owner of the field sent in a great big diesel tractor to mow the grass. Looking quite the sport, he ran over our fort, then without invitation dropped in. His eyes were big as saucers when he popped back over the brim. The poor man looked bewildered as he climbed back out of the hole. Then a lady said, pointing her finger, 'Look, he's covered in dirt like a mole.'

"As you can imagine, by now a big crowd had gathered, including Bobby's mom and dad. Everybody seemed to be in a happy mood, but I noticed his dad had his eye on us. We were hanging around the fringes of the crowd to keep out of the way. People in the crowd said right out loud that they were having a great 'field day.'

"There was a fire hall across the street and down a little way from our house. Well, what a surprise. Suddenly, the doors banged open and out came the fire engine with its great big bell clanging and banging as it roared down the street. The firemen had their helmets and coats on, waving their big axes. They were headed for the field to save the day. Then, wonder of wonders, two great big towing trucks arrived and started moving people out of the way. They drove onto the field and each put a big hook down into the hole and hooked onto the tractor. As they started their winches, the tractor slowly appeared above the hole and, boy, did all the people ever cheer.

"We had a great time, but it's still not quite the end. There's no doubt, my friend, that these boys were in for a scare. In the crowd, Mom and Dad had their eye on my lad, so for Dad's anger he had to prepare. When they all got back home, Dad and Bob went alone, and with my paws I covered my ears. Back from the shed, without supper to bed, I slept with him, licking his tears.

"I couldn't usually sleep in bed with Bobby, but tonight was a little different. Bobby and me lay there quite a long time, feeling pretty hungry. Then we saw a light under the door. Before long, in came Bobby's Mom with food for us both, but she made us wait. Bobby had to say grace before we gobbled down our dinner. He got out of bed, on his knees, said his prayers, and I sat down beside him to try. We asked Jesus for grace, I saw tears on his face, then Mom kissed us and started to cry."

Now, for a dog, you have to admit that Eugene writes a pretty good story.

*Agnes Mary as 9 month old baby
in England in 1925*

*Agnes Mary with her father
in 1928, age 3*

Chapter Two

JANUARY 20, 1925, DAWNED WATERY GREY, struggling to bring light through the heavy, smog-laden air of Birmingham. The front door opened on one of a long line of council houses on Brandhall Lane in the suburb of Quinton, ejecting Agnes Mary, the first and oldest of William and Ellen Edmonds' four children onto the street and off to school. The exact house number has faded from memory, but for our purposes it matters not. To the casual observer, all the houses were identical and house numbers were necessary for postal delivery and that sort of thing.

Agnes Mary was a gangly, sprightly, dark-haired girl destined to become a babysitter for all the subsequent babies her mother would bear. To Agnes

Mary's recollection, her family seemed to move to a new house every year. Whatever the reason, the consequence is that Agnes Mary didn't stay long enough in one place to establish permanent friendships. This probably suited her mother well, for all of Agnes Mary's free time was spent babysitting her sister and two brothers until her dad came home from work.

Her dominant childhood memory was of not feeling loved, though the family pet seemed to be. When babies would come, Dad and Mom would jump around with joy. Mom would love to change their little bums; Dad would be happy, whether it was a girl or boy. A year or two later, Mom would get blue, the novelty having worn off. Another baby would be coming, too, and this one might have a cough. The older one was seven now and couldn't do nuthin' right. Mom and Dad were always mad and always seemed to fight. Her mother talked down to her. "You really are no good. Why do you have to be so dim? Your head is solid wood."

She couldn't use as an excuse the fact that times were bad. Listen to the terms they used: "Mom's kitty," "dog and Dad." They'd say, "You're Mommy's baby pussy cat, and Mommy loves you so. Mommy doesn't know what she would do if ever you should go." Or "You're Daddy's little poochy poo, you're such a peachy pet. We love it, sleeping next to you, when in our bed you get." If some folks would treat their kids like their dogs and cats, the kids might think the parents had blown their lids and stop being brats.

Mother Ellen Edmonds was a raven-haired woman of Irish descent with a peppery temper. Irish people with dark hair were called "the Black Irish," a reflection on their Spanish heritage. She and her husband William were not drinkers. When William came home each day from his work as administrator of the porters at Dudley Road Hospital, he would see to the four kids with supper, then later put them to bed. The rest of the evening he would spend reading, and perhaps listening to news on the radio.

This arrangement, of course, might leave you wondering where the mother of the house was. This was a question that Agnes Mary, in her innocent youth, could not answer. She only knew that her mother was not there most days when she and her siblings came home from school. But on pain of a beating, Agnes Mary had to be there as a surrogate mom. Mother Edmonds was a woman of strong social bent and found more fulfillment in socializing than mothering. This led inevitably to friction with her husband, and Agnes Mary was witness to physical abuse in the home when tempers flared. Indeed, on one occasion a beautiful black eye decorated her mother's countenance.

However, we must not judge Ellen and William— or anyone else, for that matter—based on casual observation. We must leave these matters to the One who will judge all flesh.

Agnes Mary's father William was a handsome dark-haired Englishman who, as the story has it, fudged his age to enlist in the British army at fifteen to fight in the First World War. After suffering a leg wound, he was shipped home to recuperate and was rejected by his mother, dad, and sister. The story seems to carry some truth because his personality became very stiff and unemotional. Agnes Mary remembers that throughout her young life, she did not receive any warmth or love from either her mom or dad, though her sister Joan ("the pretty one") and brother Doug seemed to fare much better in that regard. Her recollection is that her family life was spent looking in from outside and feeling that she wasn't part of the family. She vowed that she would move out on her own at the first opportunity, a reflection of the independent, self-reliant spirit slowly developing in her.

It should be noted that the family, if asked, would declare to be Roman Catholic, though any activity in support of that assertion would not be sufficient to convict them in a court of law. The glue that held them in the veil was their Irish Catholic grandmother, Ellen's mother, who purposed to ascertain that her grandchildren all attended mass. When Agnes Mary was eight, her mother commissioned a neighbour woman to make a white satin dress for her first communion. This evidence of uncharacteristic motherly concern was commendable but badly tarnished by Ellen's notable absence at the event. Indeed, not one member of the family, including the grandmother, attended Agnes Mary's first communion, immeasurably strengthening her feelings of rejection.

*Bob McCluskey as public school
army cadet under retired army
Major Kirk, Principal of Jesse Ketchum
public school in Toronto
in 1936, age 10*

Chapter Three

BOB'S FOLKS MOVED FROM EAST YORK INTO TORONTO proper. Bay Street, a major north-south street gradually turns west past Bloor Street and becomes Davenport Road. The house they rented is a tall flat-roofed house at 182 Davenport. Most of the houses along that stretch are distinguished by their postage-stamp-sized front lawns, if they can boast a front lawn at all. Indeed, most front right up to the sidewalk, presenting their narrow faces to the street.

A neighbour family a little farther west, close to the intersection of Avenue Road, ran a radio repair shop called Central Radio Labs. Bob became fast friends with their youngest son, Harold Maitland. They had a lot of fun jumping over the narrow alleyways between houses.

As memory hearkens back to youth,
remember well our times at play,
with Harold jumping roof to roof,
a pastime dangerous, forsooth,
adventurous foray.

Three stories high, seen from below,
with narrow alleyways between,
the way up, city kids would know,
but wouldn't do it in the snow,
made sure we weren't seen.

We dreamed of pirates long ago,
of daring acrobats of old,
as flying over roofs we'd go,
so careful not to look below.
We were very bold.

If Mother'd known our little spoof,
of how we spent our day,
cavorting bravely roof to roof,
we'd be confined, and that's the truth,
inside the house to stay.

The school Bobby and Harold attended was called Jesse Ketchum Public School. A retired army man, Major Kirk, ran the school like an army command. Harold and Bobby, a couple of skinny kids in Grade Eight, along with several almost-sixteen-year-olds in their class were more like men and in fact worked on garbage trucks part-time until they completed their required schooling. Their idea of fun, as they marched up the stairs in the morning, was to grab the kid in front of them on the inside of the thigh. It was called a horse bite.

Now, you have to understand, there was an unwritten code of conduct: you did not cry out, or a worse fate waited after school. You just gritted your teeth, fought back tears, and kept climbing those stairs like a good soldier. You carried your bruises like badges of honour.

When Bob was almost sixteen, he met and fell in love with a beautiful girl in his class. He and Marjory grew very close. He would travel several miles to her home by bus to see her, and on more than one occasion stayed too late to catch the return bus. He would then have to walk, perhaps ten miles in the wee hours of the morning, to get home. But when you're young and in love, you'll do anything just to be with your sweetheart.

Sadly, Bob made her pregnant and her stepmother somehow induced a miscarriage. Bob learned of this after the fact, although it probably would not have made any difference, though it certainly has brought him to his knees before the Lord in repentance years later. She broke Bob's young heart by later throwing him over for a young army officer.

Harold was learning to repair radios with his dad part-time, and Bob was at his house a lot. The first time he saw Harold's bedroom, what a surprise he had. In Harold's room, the drawers were open. You couldn't have shocked him more, for the neat rows upon rows of folded clothes made it look like he slept in a store. Later on he found out why Harold's shirts were so neat, with a paper band around each one. His dad hated the smell of laundry soap in the house, so they sent the laundry out and it came back like new.

Bob had a sad surprise one day when they were seventeen. He learned that his best friend Harold had contracted tuberculosis and was sent to the Hamilton Sanatorium—for two years, as it turned out. Bob travelled to Hamilton to visit Harold a few times before other events in his life separated them.

Another incident in Bob's young life occurred during this period, although at the time, in his happy, carefree life, it was anything but sad. Through a circumstance forgotten now, Bob came through his sister into the social circles of a friend of hers: a married woman who somehow seduced him one night. The reason, as he later learned, was that she and her husband couldn't have a baby, though they had tried for many years. Though she was the aggressor in this affair, Bob was certainly not an innocent victim. The woman did become pregnant, and as a Christian later in life, Bob's greatest regret became that he had a son somewhere. It was a reason for ongoing prayer.

World War II was still tearing up the world when Bob turned seventeen in 1943. For a young man, the lure of world adventure was like waving a red flag in front of a bull. The prospect of injury or death seemed impossible to this teenager. Young men went to war without a second thought. As has been noted by wiser men, this makes armies possible. If armies were drawn from the ranks of fifty- or sixty-year-olds, debate would be endless; ultimately wisdom would prevail and the real or imagined affront be forgiven and forgotten.

But back to reality. At seventeen and a half, Bob took the streetcar downtown to the Royal Canadian Air Force recruiting centre at Wellington and Bay Street. Without further ado, he found himself wearing Air Force blue.

In 1943, with war all over the world, Bob was wet behind the ear, with no conception of fear and wanting some action bad. The RCAF was looking for boys to be wireless air gunners. He paid them a visit, they invited him in, and asked if he'd started to shave. After they'd had their little joke, they got down to business, took a few of them into another room, and ordered them to peel down to the buff. If that wasn't enough, they had to bend over and cough, checking places they never knew they had, and then put back on the clothes they'd taken off.

Off to the barber they marched en masse, trying hard not to fall out of step. Bob was not a hair stylist, we hasten to add, but at scalping he showed lots of pep. Into another building they marched, where their superiors started throwing them clothes. How they were able to size up the boys at a glance, heaven only knows.

A nice sergeant then billeted them at the Horse Palace at the Canadian National Exhibition. In two attractive cots in horse stalls, they were feeling quite perplexed. After a week in that dampness and cold, Bob started to feel quite sick. They transferred him quick to Chorley Park Military Hospital.

He was diagnosed with bronchial asthma and given a hospital stay. What a pain. He would never again see all his newfound friends in the RCAF. He soon got well, but the condition was chronic and he now had weak eyes, so they threw him out. Bob's experience in the Air Force was rather brief. Our fresh-faced prospective warrior found himself escorted unceremoniously out the back door of the RCAF selection centre at a place called Little Norway. With a war still in progress, he found himself once more a civilian.

Around this time, Bob once more fell in love, this time with his friend Harold's niece, Helen, a buxom blonde beauty. After making him her star-struck lover, with intentions of marriage, she dropped him like a hot potato for an older man, a butcher who worked in the same store as her mother. She eventually married him and had a lot of kids, Bob later learned.

During his brief tenure in the Air Force, Bob became friends with Henry Rood, a young man from Canada's east coast. Henry had also been rejected by the RCAF and, salving the wounds of rejection, they joined forces.

Bob took Henry home with him for a few days to decide what to do next.

At the recommendation of Bob's cousin Joe Gans, he and Henry hitchhiked from Toronto to Montreal, where they hoped to ship out on a freighter to see the world. Embarking on an adventure of this stature with little or no resources does, in retrospect, elicit fear and trepidation, but not for two eighteen-year-olds in the middle of a world war.

Fickle fate again played a hand in our hero's adventures, subjecting both boys to rejection once more at the Merchant Navy's hiring hall. No experience meant no hire. The boys then separated; Bob polished up his trusty thumb and, in the middle of winter, bravely set out back to Toronto.

Many details regarding this return trip have faded into the mists of time but one event Bob will never forget. Somewhere east of Toronto, perhaps near Belleville, we find our hero in the middle of a cold snowy night, vainly trying to hitch a ride on an empty highway. Almost all of the old Highway 2, in those days, was unilluminated. In the pitch black night, Bob had to find some shelter. Feeling his way, he stumbled upon what turned out to be an old-fashioned motel, tiny cottages with a separate unheated outhouse to service them all. Penniless and desperate to get out of the cold, Bob locked himself inside the smelly outhouse and fell asleep hunched up with his chin on his knees.

How long he slept, he had no way of knowing, but he was driven groggily back into semi-consciousness by incessant pounding on the door. He unlocked the door and stumbled half-awake through an angry group of large, full-bladdered ladies shouting and gesticulating outside. Finding his way back onto the highway, he proceeded to walk westward, knowing that ultimately, if he survived, the lights of Toronto would appear.

With no traffic at that time of night, Bob was excited to see car lights approaching. He bravely stepped out onto the road and stuck out his thumb. He was hardly able to contain his joy and relief as the car came to a stop. He grasped the door handle and, opening the door, slipped into the luxurious warmth.

The driver, dressed in pyjamas and a house coat, began to make conversation. As Bob slowly warmed up, the man began to explain his situation and where he was heading. Whether or not you, the reader, believe that God sometimes injects himself into man's affairs, Bob certainly does. The man explained that he was the owner of the motel. After he'd gotten the ladies calmed down, he had gone to his house, picked up a little change, and proceeded to drive down the road in the direction he'd seen Bob take, hoping to intercept him.

"I've had my share of tough times, and now I'm able to give a little back," he said. "I'll drive you to the next town where there is an all-night diner. From there, you might get a lift to Toronto. Here's a couple of bucks to get something to eat. God bless you, son."

Was that God or what? Bob had caused this man to get out of bed on a blustery cold night to mollify a gaggle of angry ladies. Then, instead of getting back into his warm bed, the man had gotten into his car out and, just on chance, started down the road to try to find and help this kid who had caused all of the night's problems, not to berate him but to comfort and help him. Yep, that's God.

The rest of that trip home is forgotten now, but after licking his wounds and resting on Mom's home cooking for a while, Bob determined to find work on Great Lakes shipping, since he couldn't go to sea.

Soon he was off on another hitchhiking adventure to Montreal, where he joined up once more with Henry. Together they visited the Merchant's Marines hiring hall and found berths on the same small canaler, so called because, unlike huge upper-lake grain carriers, she could go through all the locks between Head of the Lakes and Quebec. They were hired on as trimmers. The trimmer's job was to assist the fireman.

Rejected by the Air Force,
they hitch-hiked to Montreal
to try the Merchant Navy.
They went to the hiring hall.

Rejection again, no experience,
so they couldn't go to sea,
but they'd hire them on the lake boats.
Trimmers they would be.

They both signed on to the William Schupp,
a canaller, ten thousand tons,
a coal burner, two boilers, four fires for steam.
That's the way she runs.

Four hours on, four hours off,
each day around the clock,
firemen would clean two fires a shift,
keep up steam, however she'd rock.

They picked her up at the Welland Canal,
and now they're adventure bound,
at the end of the season, through terrible storm,
she'd lay up in Owen Sound.

She'd haul coal from Quebec to Thunder Bay,
though she's only a little ship,
bring back wheat through the Welland Canal,
where she's small enough to fit.

She'd coal up at Sandusky, Ohio,
on the American side,
they're on the way to Thunder Bay
in the fire hold, stripped to the hide.

There the fireman started pulling fires,
one under each boiler... each watch,
as he pulls hot coals out onto the deck,
takes a swig from a mickey of scotch.

Their job's to pour buckets of water,
on the coals so he's able to toil,
over hot clinkers, the fire rebuild,
so the steam will continue to boil.

They shovel clinkers into the ash guns,
and they're pumped out over the side,
in the storm later on with no covers,
those two holes were open wide.

The storm that we're referring to
was December, 1944.
With gale force winds and record snow,
Ontario suffered sore.

In Toronto, people skied to work,
a streetcar was blown on its side.
On Lake Superior, sailing for home,
their ship almost turned on its side.

With hearts in their mouths, she righted herself,
rolling with the next wave,
on her beams end, bow up to the sky,
she'll be finished, if hatches cave.

As she shudders and shakes, fights for her life,
waves break over the ship.
Ice continues to build, if top heavy she gets,
this could easily make her flip.

While down in the fire hold, stripped to the waist,
it looked like a scene from hell.
From those sizzling clinkers, clouds of steam;
bad trouble if pressure fell.

Lake water pours out on the fire hold floor,
from those open holes on the side,
soaking the coal that they have to use,
causing steam pressure to slide.

Vague figures obscured by steamy mist,
as they toil to keep pressure up,
for if headway they lose, sideways she'll turn...
the end of the William Schupp.

At the end of their watch, they have to climb up,
to the after house with fear,
not out on the deck, they'd be swept away,
they can judge the waves from up here.

With the roll of the ship, the starboard submerged,
the port side cabin door was dry.
Then they'd drop to the deck, race around to the door,
and had to be pretty spry.

They'd unlock from within, to let you in,
but one time they were too slow.
The ship rolled back again, had a grip of pain,
held his breath, 'cause under he'd go.

But it worked out all right; you can tell he survived,
as they slowly headed for port.
That guy finished his mickey,
for sure when they dock he'll find himself a quart.

As they swaggered ashore, people stared with awe,
at the ice built up on their ship.
But they acted as if it was nothing at all.
Nt to worry... just part of the trip.

Agnes Mary in English Army
in 1944 at age 19

Agnes Mary,
third from right
with friends in 1944, age 19

Agnes Mary on left of
buddy and pastor in 1944,
age 19

Chapter Four

AGNES MARY'S CHILDHOOD DID NOT HOLD MANY good memories for her. In fact, she has practically no memories of childhood fun times. Because of her mother's constant absence, she was forced to assume responsibility for smothering—or rather, mothering—her three siblings after school. Many years later, her younger brother Doug told her husband that as kids they would bring any problem to Agnes Mary and she would fix it, giving her a surprised feeling of pride later in life.

When she was about fourteen, on September 1, 1939, England entered World War II against Germany. Food rationing was implemented immediately and a long period of deprivation began for Agnes Mar—and, of course, the whole of Britain. Some families seemed to fare better than others, due in part to the kitchen skills of some British mothers. Unfortunately for Agnes Mary, her mother was abysmally lacking in that department and her children grew increasingly skinny and hungry. Mother Ellen. strangely enough, managed to maintain her customary plump appearance.

For two more years during the war, Agnes Mary and her siblings continued with school. Cities around them were bombed, and they became used to seeing enemy aircraft overhead.

Once or twice, bombs dropped in their immediate vicinity and they had to run and duck into bomb shelters like rabbits going to ground. On one occasion when she and her sister Joan were walking home from school down a country road, they were strafed by a German fighter aircraft and had to dive unceremoniously into the ditch. For some reason, this event was forgotten. Years later, her sister couldn't believe that Agnes Mary's memory of that event was completely blank.

Back then, children were required to attend school until the age of sixteen, after which any further education had to be paid for. Agnes Mary was a very good student and took the entrance exam for a business college, passing with flying colours. Her mother had promised that they would fund her education if she did well, but sadly, when the time came Ellen either would not or could not fulfill that promise, much to Agnes Mary's disappointment, for she loved school.

England had a system for both boys and girls to apprentice with a company to receive hands-on training in a chosen field. Though this paid very little at first, it benefited both companies and the young people starting out. This was the next logical step for Agnes Mary, just fresh out of school. After submitting applications to several companies, she was accepted as an office apprentice by Guest, Keen and Nettlefolds, a large steel manufacturing company with many different shops and offices. After working there for a couple of years, she was conscripted for ammunition factory work. Because she was reluctant to go and delayed reporting in, she was dressed down and warned that she had better obey the order or risk being shot as a traitor. Needless to say, she did respond. Though she hated that work, she stayed for about six months, until an opportunity arose to join the British Women's Army—or ATS, the Auxiliary Territorial Service—where she very quickly found herself stationed at the Chilwell army depot, just outside the city of Nottingham, as a clerk/typist in the deputy commander's office.

Agnes Mary has fond memories of these times of great camaraderie and fun. On one particular evening, she went with some of her bunkmates to a dance at the Palais de Dance in Nottingham. Now, remember that we're speaking here about an innocent twenty-one-year-old girl who had hardly ever kissed a man in her life.

Before the evening had ended, a tall, handsome, thirty-year-old pilot came over and asked for a dance.

Stasiek was a career Polish Air Force officer who had transferred to the Royal Air Force before the war. As Agnes Mary was to subsequently learn, he was married to a British woman, had one child, and they were supposedly seeking a divorce. Stasiek was, it seems, smitten with this striking young woman; having learned where she was stationed, he would wait at the depot gate to drive her and court her for days after. Agnes Mary was flattered by this attention, and before very long she found herself with him almost every weekend, trysting at a local bed and breakfast. He proclaimed his love for her and that he would soon divorce his wife and marry her. This went on for five years and was beginning to wear a little thin towards the end.

When a girlfriend invited Agnes Mary to go on a blind date, because she was disappointed and disillusioned with Stasiek, she accepted. Werner was a handsome and athletic German Jew who with his parents had fled Germany just before the war with almost nothing. His father had been wealthy and prosperous in Germany, owning several businesses, and Werner had embarked on an education to become a doctor. A surgeon, in fact. All of this had been lost and they now lived in Birmingham where they were endeavouring to start a textile factory.

When he landed on Agnes Mary's doorstep that spring evening in 1951, he was twenty-nine and she was twenty-six. They gradually became good friends and the relationship quickly grew from friends to lovers. The consequence of this romance was that she became pregnant. When she revealed this to Werner, he wanted very much to marry her, but Agnes Mary would not accept. As fond as she was of Werner, she felt that she didn't love him enough to marry him, and in any case, she had never met his parents. Because she was not Jewish, she knew this would not work.

Six months after the war ended, Agnes Mary had been discharged from the Service. After working for various companies, she eventually became employed in the offices of the Docker Bros. Paint Company, where she became supervisor of the typing pool. But when her pregnancy threatened to reveal itself, she resigned. The reason she gave was that she planned to emigrate to either Australia or Canada. Because the company prized her very highly, they tried to persuade her to stay. The prospective emigration was, in fact, true, and that was exactly what happened almost two years later. In any event, in those days she wouldn't have been allowed to continue as a pregnant single woman.

During her pregnancy and after, Werner was very supportive, not only financially but emotionally as well. This continued right up to her departure for Canada, as he provided additional financial aid for the trip.

Agnes Mary lived at home during these years and continued to do so after her pregnancy, right up until she boarded the boat. Her parents provided a home for her throughout the good and not so good times, and tribute must be paid to their constancy and reliability in those years.

Bob McCluskey,
private in army in 1944, age 18

Chapter Five

ON THEIR LAST TRIP THROUGH THE LOCKS AT THE Welland Canal, a sack of mail was delivered to the ship for the crew. Bob received an invitation from Canada's federal government asking if he would kindly consider joining a bunch of lovely lads in the Canadian Army. Anxious to comply, he boarded a bus from Owen Sound for Toronto after they'd laid up the ship for the winter.

The army welcomed him with open arms, and before long he was on his way to Camp Borden where he was subjected to three months of intensive basic training. Just as he was finishing, on May 8, 1945, V-E (Victory in Europe) Day was declared. They were all given the choice of receiving a discharge or volunteering for the Pacific Theatre of War. Demonstrating the undeniable wisdom of a teenager, Bob chose the latter and was soon on his way to Brantford, where he began a three-month program of advanced training. As this training program was nearing completion, on August 15, 1945, V-J (Victory in Japan) Day was declared.

Well, that was that. The war was over so it was time to get a discharge and get back to civvy life. Not so fast. The demob (demobilization) facilities would be needed to discharge the vets coming home, so the Johnnies-come-lately would just have to wait. Fair enough. So what to do with them? Why, attach them to the Veterans Guard of Canada, guarding prisoners of war, of course. Bob and a whole carload of newly trained recruits found themselves ejected from the train at a base lumber camp deep in the bush one hundred miles north of Sault Ste. Marie on the Tamiskaming and Northern Ontario Railway (T&NO).

They all bunked down at midnight for a few hours in a large log cabin with two-tier bunks lining the walls. In the centre of the room was an oil drum on its side, converted into a wood stove. The temperature that night was −40 degrees Fahrenheit and the inside walls were covered with frost despite the bright, cherry-red stove a-dancin', an old bushwhacker feeding it sap-filled pine logs. That heat never reached the room's perimeters, even though the fireman had to keep back from the stove's intense heat. At about three in the morning, a caterpillar tractor pulled up front hauling a sleigh load of baled hay. Their platoon was rousted up to pile on the sled. Then they were off on a ten-mile logging road to a distant bush camp.

Let's paint a picture of this bizarre scene. The tractor had a sheet metal cowling that funnelled all the engine heat around the driver to keep him warm, so he was okay. The soldiers, on the other hand, were either sitting or lying on hard solid blocks of baled hay out in the open. They wore steel-hobnailed army boots and army-issue uniforms suited to a kinder, more southern clime. They had to jump off the tractor and keep up on foot just to keep warm. That would have been okay—after all, they were healthy teenagers for the most part—if it hadn't been for the fact that the tractor travelled at a pace between a fast walk and a slow trot. They could fast-walk or slow-trot, holding onto the tailgate, but before too long they would begin to breathe heavily as the cold air cut into their lungs like a knife.

About halfway to the bush camp, they came to a hill too steep for the tractor to pull the sled up and over, which caused a delay. The driver had to unhook the sled, connect a cable to the sled from the drum on the back of the tractor, and drive the tractor up the hill, unravelling cable as he went. When he was over the brow of the hill, he locked the drum and drove down the other side, pulling the sled to the top.

Their platoon was commanded by a Veterans Guard sergeant, a leathery-faced older man of Canadian-Indian descent who knew the bush. He decided that too much time would be lost waiting for that manoeuvre to be completed, and they would slowly freeze just standing around. So after getting directions, as these old tote roads tended to branch off confusingly, he gave the command for them to just start walking and let the tractor catch up with them farther down the road.

Bob carried graphic memories of that cold night's walk for the rest of his life. The moon was brilliant in the snapping cold, their footsteps crunching loudly as they walked. Every now and then they would hear what sounded like a loud rifle shot, startling them in the forest's stillness.

The sergeant smiled when he saw the surprise on their young faces. "Not to worry, boys," he said. "When it gets this cold, the sap sometimes freezes right in the tree and the expansion can blow a large tree apart."

With that reassurance, they walked on through the frozen night.

They started to hear wolves howling, first on the right and then on the left, keeping pace with them. This was eerie and the bush-wise sergeant explained that a pack of wolves was tracking them, signalling each other. But they rarely attacked humans, especially a group as large as theirs. While this was reassuring information, the soldiers couldn't help looking over their shoulders and closing ranks a little.

As a testimony to the reality of wolves in the bush, Bob was later called on to shoot a horse that had foundered. The horses hauled logs and this one couldn't get back up after falling down. It would have been inhumane to leave him through the night for the wolves to eat. Bob hated to have to do it, but graphic evidence reassured him the next morning that he had done the right thing. They found the horse frozen solid, its whole hindquarters completely eaten away. Not many days later, there was nothing left of him but bones.

The tractor never did catch up, and as dawn broke they heard dogs barking ahead of them, heralding their arrival in camp. They soon settled in to a daily routine of escorting German prisoners of war to cut trees to be used for lumber and pulp—mostly pulp, because of their size.

Looking back on this experience, Bob came to realize that, though he was armed, he had been just a kid and most of the prisoners were older men. Had they so desired, they could easily have overpowered and disarmed him. However, these men knew that the war was lost and they would be returned home soon enough. Also, they were so deep in the bush that there was really no place to go anyway.

The prisoners at this camp were mostly navy men, almost all submariners. When they'd been brought to POW camps in Canada, they had been given the choice to work and be paid a little in credit, or stay behind barbed wire for the duration. The diehard Nazis would have refused to work and regarded those who did as traitors, but the men Bob was guarding were living a very healthy life. They were fed just as well as any Canadian lumberman. Working outside in forty-below weather gave those men enormous appetites, and they were fed all they could eat. Bob knew this because he and the other soldiers were fed by the same cook in the same cookhouse with the same food.

One thing Bob learned there was that lumber camp cooks were king of their domain. Breakfast would consist of great enamelled platters of fried eggs and bacon on the table with more to come as the tray was emptied. There was toast, of course, and steaming coffee. After that, trays of sliced apple pie until you could eat no more. Those cooks brought good food and lots of it.

Ah! Appetite, fair appetite
Young lads' insatiable delight.
With hungry eyes digesticating
The groaning board's largess.
Young frames voraciously
demanding copious
quantities outstanding,
fuelling inner racing engine,
where it hides, we only guess.

Those cooks ruled the cookhouse with an iron fist. No talking was allowed. The men were to just eat fast and quiet and get out so that the next shift could be seated, and this was strictly enforced. If you insisted on talking after you were warned once, you were thrown out and that was that. Needless to say, hungry men learn quick.

Though they earned a small amount of credit, they weren't given any money. They made skis in their spare time and bought ski harnesses by mail order from the Eaton's catalogue—as well as tobacco, candy, and anything else that could not be used to escape. Some of the prisoners were skillful at building ships in bottles and tried to sell these to the guards. This was, of course, forbidden, since they were not allowed to be given Canadian money. Because of Canada's fair treatment of POWs, it would not be surprising if the credit balance they had earned was given to them in German Marks when they were sent home.

Bob's sojourn in the great white north came to an end later that year. When the war in the Pacific ended, the camps were disbanded, the prisoners sent back to Germany, the Veterans Guard demobilized, and Bob's band of young recruits sent back to Toronto to be discharged.

That midnight adventure jogging through the bush badly affected Bob's lungs. Later in life, he received a disability pension from Veterans Affairs. Canada does look after its veterans very well.

*Beautiful Agnes Mary
in England after war
in 1945, age 20*

Chapter Six

WE FIND AGNES MARY AT THE RAIL OF THE OCEAN liner *S.S. Samaria*, gazing down on the dock at Southampton, about to embark for Canada holding her one-year-old daughter Jannette in her arms. On the dock, she could see both her mother and father waving goodbye. When she saw her father put both hands over his face and weep, she thought he was weeping at the loss of his granddaughter, for he had become quite fond of her. It wasn't until many years later, after her father's death, that she learned from Jannette that he had been, in fact, weeping for Agnes Mary. How Jeannette gained that information, we do not know—perhaps from the Holy Spirit, or it could have been gleaned from a conversation with her grandfather or grandmother when she was older after they moved to Canada as well.

We can only imagine the whirlwind of emotions that swirled through Agnes Mary's head, and indeed her heart, as she said goodbye to everything and everyone she had known all her life. Here was a single mother, all alone, carrying a totally dependent one-year-old baby, facing an ocean voyage to a new and alien land in which the only soul she knew was an old buddy, Peggy, from her munitions factory days. Peggy had become a war bride and made the same voyage not long after the war ended to join her new husband in Saskatoon, Saskatchewan. Peggy and Agnes Mary had stayed in touch, and when Peggy learned that Agnes Mary desired to relocate to Canada, she agreed to sponsor her.

The *S.S. Samaria* docked in Montreal after twelve days at sea. There, Agnes Mary found herself, with a squalling and hungry baby, at the end of a long line waiting to go through customs. A St. John Ambulance attendant came and took the baby to a small area set up for that sort of thing while her mother, with all her luggage, went through customs. These people were a great help in a time of need. Once safely through customs, Agnes Mary found the train which would take her all the way to Saskatoon.

Soon they were off again, on a four-day trip halfway across Canada.

Agnes Mary and Jannette slept together in a curtained lower bunk in a sleeper car and went to dinner together for each meal. The waiter brought the same dinner for each, but they cut up Jannette's food real fine. This was the routine all the way across Canada's heartland until that happy day in July 1953 when they finally arrived at the station platform in Saskatoon. A travel-weary Agnes Mary was met by Peggy and husband Jack, who welcomed them warmly and took them to their home where they would stay for about a month.

An unknown destiny awaited our transplanted English lovely in that Saskatchewan city, but first she had to get a job. She did so the next day, at a large local company. After a month with Peggy, Agnes Mary found a place to rent where the landlady—by coincidence also called Peggy—agreed to babysit Jannette. For the next year, Agnes Mary bussed to work every day and experienced winter days of −40 degrees, waiting at bus stops morning and night. Winter snow was not beyond her experience, but she had never in her life imagined anything so cold.

After about a year, her destiny began to materialize. Through a series of circumstances, she changed jobs and began to work at Saskatoon's police headquarters. She was not there long before a tall and handsome police officer named Fred Martin began to show an interest in her. Because of her job, Agnes Mary had access to the records; when she checked Fred's records, she found that he was married but legally separated with full custody of two very young daughters who were staying with his mom and dad at a place called The Pas in northern Manitoba. After her five-year experience with Stasiek in England, Agnes Mary didn't want to again be involved with a married man and wouldn't allow any encouragement. But Fred was very persistent. He waited for her to finish work every afternoon, then drove her home and waited outside her house in the morning to drive her back to work. He plied her with flowers and chocolates and many kindnesses, and gradually wore down her resistance. They began to keep company very seriously and did eventually marry after Fred's divorce was finalized one and a half years later. As the fairy tale says, destiny was fulfilled.

A few months before they wed, Fred promised to build her a house and promptly bought a lot and began to build a cement block house. After they married, they rented a house just down the street from the lot so he could conveniently work on the new house in his spare time, but even then it took four years. Meanwhile, a year after they were married, they brought Fred's two young daughters to live with them. Their new family was up and running.

Our fertile heroine Agnes Mary became pregnant soon after they married, and their son Rick was added to their growing family. Five years later, their second son, Gerald, came along. They were in their new house by this time. A final child, their lovely daughter Jennifer, was born five years after that in the spring of 1965, completing their family of four girls and two boys.

During these married years, Agnes Mary sometimes worked out of the house, but with so many children at home from the start, it made more sense to stay home and take in boarders. At one point soon after their marriage, they had five young students boarding with them. This helped a great deal with household expenses but added more work. Their own children were still too young to be of much help around the house and required much of her time and attention.

Because of coming events, a review at this point would be helpful. Agnes Mary's life in England and onward seemed to follow a succession of stressful and often traumatic experiences, beginning with a home life which imposed entirely too much responsibility upon a child so young, essentially robbing her of her childhood. Then, just as she was growing into freedom from those years of restraint, the war broke out with its stresses and dangers, not to mention deprivation and shortage of food and the loss of young neighbour men she knew who went away to war and ceased to exist.

An interesting sidelight to those days of rationing is the fact that for the rest of her life, Agnes Mary could not enjoy anything that was too salty or too sweet, qualities which most of us regard as desirable and tasty. She could not enjoy them because the flavours were too intense. When she first arrived in Canada, everyday sliced bread seemed like sweet cake to her.

Coming back to our account of Agnes Mary's early married life with Fred, we look in on a very busy and harried housewife with four children so far, five young boarders, and a loving and attentive policeman husband on shift work.

While Fred did as much as he could do to help out around the house, the burden of her acquired household was a heavy one. With so many mouths to feed and all the associated cooking, washing, and organizing, the stress was too much and Agnes Mary began to have an emotional breakdown. Because she had such a strong personality, she found it difficult to understand her frequent, sudden crying fits and the unhappiness that plagued her. Her doctor told her that this was common with war brides and prescribed tranquilizers, but after a month of feeling like a zombie she gave them up.

During this breakdown, which lasted two years, the family attended the local Anglican church. Agnes Mary had been raised as a Roman Catholic and Fred as an Anglican, so they agreed to worship God as Anglicans and enjoyed that church very much. The pastor was married with children, and although his family was often plagued with sickness, he frequently visited Agnes Mary during her illness. He would just sit with her at the kitchen table and quietly hold her hand. He talked very little, just prayed silently. She received great comfort from his ministering and to this day thanks God for his healing help.

After a year of illness, and at the end of another school year, Agnes Mary felt that if she could work outside the home, the change might help her. With the student boarders gone for the summer, she made arrangements with an older lady across the road to babysit the children whenever Fred's shift prevented him from doing so. Without further ado, she was off to find a job and promptly met with success.

Her recovery lent some credence to her theory that outside work might help. With her healing came a renewed interest in life, along with a return to her old vitality. When she expressed a desire to sew, Fred bought her a sewing machine. Knowing nothing at all about sewing, she took the machine completely apart on the living room rug and assembled it back together again. Now familiar with it, she began to sew clothes for the kids. She even learned how to sew great business outfits for herself.

One day, Agnes Mary could not insert the bobbin in her sewing machine. After purchasing a new one, she discovered that the old bobbin was jammed in. With great difficulty, Fred was able to extract it; he then returned the new bobbin. The culprit turned out to be their three-year-old son, Gerald. With his active imagination, he had been trying to help his mom. When Fred was working on something and tightening screws, Gerald would follow behind, helping his dad by unloosening the screws again. Fred was very puzzled, because he was certain he had tightened them.

Before Gerald could talk very well, he used an expression his mom didn't understand.

There once was a three-year-old slip of a lad.
When he finally talked, all the family were glad.
His mother was puzzled when he tried to speak,
from his big sisters four, explanation she'd seek.
"What's he saying?"
we'd hear puzzled Mother exclaim
when strange words he's repeating again and again.

Of course, Gerald knew what he was trying to say
with his expletive uttered "Fer-Diddle-Dar-Dey."
He'd "fer-diddle-dar" this and "fer-diddle-dar" that
when, with his older brother, he'd get in a spat.
When his big sisters tried with authority to speak,
he'd "fer-diddle-dar" them, then a safe haven seek.

Now he's finally grown up,
new expression he's learned,
language greatly improved,
from diplomas he's earned.
This childish expression must soon fade away,
But somewhere out in the ether... fer-diddle-dar-dey.

We have now arrived at the year 1965. Around this time, Fred was transferred from the Traffic Division, which he loved, to the Morality Division, which he grew increasingly to hate, to the point where it affected his emotional health. His captain, knowing that Fred was at the point of quitting, suggested that he take a full year off to recover. Then, when he came back, the captain promised that he'd put him in charge of Traffic. They valued Fred that much.

But it was too late. Fred had lost all interest in pursuing a police career any further. To save his emotional and mental health, and with Agnes Mary's compassionate agreement, Fred resigned.

Chapter Seven

BOB'S ARRIVAL BACK IN TORONTO WAS UNHERALDED, to put it in the kindest terms. Before he could discard his uniform, it was necessary to buy some new clothes. He seemed to have outgrown anything he could find in his closet. So now, what to do? He was completely untrained in any skills that could benefit him commercially, but he had heard of a government program to help returning veterans with various forms of education and technical training. He checked this out and selected a course in sign-writing which he felt artistically drawn to, if you'll pardon the pun. After completion of the course, he made application to the Coca-Cola Company in their sign department. Happily, he was accepted.

He found himself working under the department head, a Mr. Art Tier, cutting out stencils used to silkscreen the customer's lettering on storefront signs with Coca-Cola advertising. Additionally, and much more importantly, he gradually became assistant to Mr. Tier, answering his office phone and composing and writing his business letters, etc., when he wasn't at his bench cutting out stencils.

Bob enjoyed this job very much and was beginning to make more money than he ever had before. With his now more durable heart recovering from a woman's unkind ministrations, this young man who was barely out of teenage years and with a healthy—perhaps some would say unhealthy—lust for life, was off and running on a busy, partying, hard-drinking social life which often lasted all night. He would then go to work all day.

While employed by Coca-Cola, Bob became friends with a man in the cooler repair department, Gord Underwood. One day, Gord asked him if he would like to meet a young woman on a blind date, his wife's cousin, who was a single mom with a five-year-old daughter. Bob agreed, and before long he became close friends with Margaret, who would a year or two later become his wife.

Margaret had earlier married a young sailor during the war and set up housekeeping with him in his hometown of London, Ontario. Though they had their daughter Donna together early in the marriage, it was doomed to failure. Suffice it to say there was physical abuse, alcoholism, and infidelity. After repeated attempts at reconciliation, Margaret left him for good and retained custody of their daughter.

When Margaret and Donna both agreed to marry Bob, Margaret had to work to finalize her divorce. This eventually made it necessary, for legal reasons, for Margaret to pay to bring her husband Art down to Toronto, and then for she and Bob to drive Art back to London in Bob's car. Bob recalls that the long drive back was fraught with tension and nervousness. However, that unpleasant chapter came to an end, as all things must, and the road was cleared for Margaret and Bob to marry. Not long after that, Bob legally adopted Donna and she grew up in her new family loved by Bob indistinguishably from her sister, who came along some years later.

When they first married, this little family of three moved into Margaret's aunt's basement apartment on South Edgely Street in Scarborough, a suburb of Toronto, until they were able to purchase a frame house from a family friend on Bush Drive in West Hill a few years later.

Margaret's uncle Walter, her dad's brother, was in charge of truck maintenance at the Brewers Warehousing Company. This company was, and may still be, the sole public and commercial provider of beer for the whole of Ontario. The company is unique in that it is non-profit, being collectively owned and funded by all the competing breweries in Ontario. These breweries support the company's operations by each paying a toll on every case of their product sold.

Margaret interceded with Uncle Walter to see if he could be influential in helping Bob find employment there, for they were a very well-paying company. Walter was kind enough to do this for Bob and Margaret. On the promise of employment the next week, Bob resigned from the Coca-Cola Company.

There was, however, an unexpected delay of several months before he could start work, and this left Bob in a tight spot. After some searching, he found employment with Lake Simcoe Ice and Fuel, driving an ice truck and delivering blocks of ice in a canvas bag on his shoulder. This was in 1956 when people still used ice boxes, albeit not many. For those who have not had the pleasure of using an ice box, they were made of wood with a door on the front through which to place the ice; there was a larger door below for food. A drain pipe ran from the ice compartment down to a deep pan that slid underneath and which had to be dumped regularly on pain of a flood. Bob's hand-freezing exercise thankfully ended three months later when he received a phone call to report for an employment interview at the Brewers Warehousing head office.

Bob was hired as a retail store employee. There were several hundred stores around the city and environs, and Bob began a career of twenty-seven years, mostly as a store manager.

Chapter Eight

THE YEAR OF 1965 SPELLED THE BEGINNING OF MAJOR change in the Martin family's relatively secure existence. The final addition to their family arrived that year, a daughter who was christened Jennifer Margaret Martin. This added expense arrived at the same time as their major source of income was abruptly terminated when Fred resigned.

Fred was not a man to just sit around, however, and he very quickly found employment selling mutual funds. Two years later, he was offered a security job at a mining company in Thompson, Manitoba, which was only a couple hours' drive from his parents in The Pas. Fred and Agnes Mary sold their house, and during the interim before possession occurred, Fred went to Thompson and found a place to rent for the family.

He then returned home and arranged for a moving company to bring all their worldly belongings in the northern city. This very clearly marked an end to their old life and opened a whole new chapter for a couple progressing rapidly into their fifties.

Because of Fred's past training and experience as a police officer, it was expected that he would be able to keep order in the mining camp, where a bunch of rough, mostly single miners lived together in company bunkhouses. These were hard-drinking, rowdy hard rock miners who made Fred's job a nightmare at times. Agnes Mary knew that she could find employment at the local hospital, but Fred wanted her to look after things at home so he could be free to develop a small business. When the time was right, Fred resigned from his security job and opened an automobile radiator repair shop. He was the kind of man who could do anything with his hands—rebuild cars or houses, or most anything else for that matter—and the business grew.

Life continued for the next three years, until in 1970 Mary Agnes's father passed away in Kitsilano, British Columbia. Her mother and father had moved there from England several years earlier to join their two sons, Doug and Bernard, and their daughter Joan. While the funeral was, of course, an unhappy time, one would think that after so many years of separation it would also have been a warm time of reunion. As Agnes Mary recalled, this was not to be. There was very little love or warmth demonstrated between her and her siblings—or, for that matter, with her mother. They had never been a close and affectionate family, and nothing seemed to have changed in that regard.

In another direction entirely, change was in the wind. Agnes Mary stayed at her mother's apartment during the funeral. This was February, and she was struck by how pleasant and warm the weather seemed, coming as she was from Thompson's forty-below temperatures. When she returned home, she lost no time in sharing this with Fred and reminding him that he had always wanted to live in B.C. As persuasive as only a wife can be, she prevailed on Fred to pull up stakes once again and move to B.C., where she felt life could be a great deal more pleasant, and perhaps even more prosperous.

Surprisingly, in view of his prospering business, Fred was immediately open to the idea. Before much time had passed, he sold his business and left by train to scout out the land in B.C. He stayed with his mother-in-law in Kitsilano while looking for a job, and found one in Vancouver working in security. After a week or so, Agnes Mary and three of their six children arrived. Fred's two daughters were by now off and married, and Agnes Mary's eldest, Janette, stayed behind with a friend.

Agnes Mary's baggage included her precious sewing machine and new vacuum cleaner, a few other prized possessions, and all their clothing in suitcases.

She had sold the rest of their belongings, bought rail fare, herded the whole gang to the train station, and brought them to Kitsilano. She did this while keeping her crew of kids dressed, fed, and happy, all on her own. Pretty resourceful.

Grandmother Ellen's apartment was suddenly overrun by five extra people, with all the attendant luggage and paraphernalia, and without exercising too much imagination, one can understand that this situation had to change, and fast. Stimulated by impending disaster, the family quickly found a house to rent in Vancouver and were able to remove all their bedlam from Grandmother's house before an explosion occurred.

The rented house also had a basement apartment, which worked out well, as their daughter Jannette, by now a lovely and talented eighteen-year-old, would be arriving soon and need the support of her family. Due to an unfortunate relationship with a boy from Thompson, Jannette would soon become a single mother.

Coming into middle age, Fred and Agnes Mary once more settled in to rebuild their lives and re-establish the family's fortunes. The kids quickly adapted to their new surroundings, as kids usually do. Fred was working five part-time jobs at the same time in those days, and one of his security assignments was for the Vancouver Port Authority. Wherever he worked, he always had his ear to the ground looking to better himself, and he was able to subject an application to the Coast Guard once he had been at the port for a while and learned the ropes. The whole family was delighted when he was accepted. No doubt Fred's excellent police training was a strong contributing factor. He then embarked on a two-year on-the-job training program. The family's new beginning was off and running.

Fred's new job gave the family much-needed security, the benefits were great, and the salary was more than they had ever hoped for. Agnes Mary began to work outside the home again and added greatly to the family fortune. As well, her trusty sewing machine came out and she began once more to make the kids clothing, and some of her own as well. Making clothing for Fred was never part of her expertise, although she did knit sweaters for him and the kids, which the kids hated and promptly lost.

Bob McCluskey,
Retail Beer Store Manager
with Brewers Warehousing Corp
from 1953 to 1980...Forfeited pension
at age 55 to honor God

Chapter Nine

BOB'S CAREER WITH THE BREWERS WAREHOUSING Company was off to a good start, and within two years he progressed from retail clerk to assistant manager, and then to store manager.

Just as Bob was established as a beer store manager, Margaret's stepmother, Mae, returned to Scotland, the place of her birth, to visit old friends. While there, she took quite ill and someone from the family had to go to her. Because Bob had several weeks of holidays due, he and Margaret agreed to go. They reserved a car at Heathrow, for they intended to drive up to Edenborough to try and make it a bit of a sightseeing trip, since neither had ever left North America, nor, incidentally, had they ever driven on the left-hand side of the road.

When they picked up the car, Bob drove out onto the ring road that encompasses London and onto the no-speed-limit M1 which runs north to Scotland.

Needless to say, he drove with extreme caution, thinking through every move and turn very carefully. That little three-cylinder engine could reach about eighty miles per hour, and though Bob's foot kept the gas pedal pinned to the floor mile after mile, Bentley and Rolls Royce limos swooshed by as if they were standing still—and on what seemed to Bob to be the wrong side.

Suddenly, the very bewildered Canadian couple ran out of highway and found themselves in a residential working class neighbourhood of some town they had never heard of. Seeking direction, Bob entered a local pub and eventually was able to understand a confusing variety of volunteered directions. While stopped, he phoned ahead to the connecting number they had been given, and to his shock and dismay learned that Mae had just passed away.

He returned to Margaret, waiting in the car, to share this sad news as gently as he could. In her grief and shock, Margaret turned weeping and began to beat on him with both arms, berating him for not flying to Scotland instead of driving as she had suggested. After the shock began to wear off, Margaret apologized and acknowledged that Bob had done the best he could.

The rest of the drive was a sad time. When they finally arrived at their destination, they were able to have a small late supper and a welcome night's rest.

Ann, the retired Scottish nurse Mae had been visiting, was very helpful with the arrangements that had to be made for Mae's funeral and burial. It was the family's wish that Mae be buried in Scotland, her first and final home. Because she was not a national of Scotland, the local police and coroner had to be involved. This took time and complicated matters a great deal, making it harder on Margaret, but finally the funeral was accomplished and Bob and Margaret were free to plan the rest of their stay.

Ann kindly suggested a drive up to the royal family's Scottish estate, Balmoral Castle, where the royal family were currently in residence. It turned out to be a lovely Sunday drive after the recent sadness. They arrived outside the castle walls and parked the car. A sparse gathering of tourists were walking around, interspersed by a few plainclothes security, each with a police dog on a leash.

It turned out that their timing was perfect. The royal family would shortly be returning from the kirk (church) in plain sight on a low nearby hill. Sure enough, before long a platoon of bagpipers and kilted soldiers appeared. They marched down the hill with three spotless black Rolls Royce limousines in close procession and very soon followed the road leading to the open castle gates. Their route brought them through the small gathering at the slow pace of the marching pipers, giving them all an exceptionally clear view of each limo occupant.

The first car contained Queen Elizabeth and Prince Phillip, graciously waving through the open window. Prince Charles and the storied Lady Diana followed, also waving but with their windows closed; this was for security reasons, as they were heirs to the throne. Sitting so tiny and demure in the end car beside a lady-in-waiting was the Queen Mum, also named Elizabeth, waving with her window down as well.

Bob and Margaret slowly wended their way to the castle gates, and they saw the gates close behind the last car. They were quite surprised at how accessible and seemingly vulnerable the royal family had been, for although there had been security, they could have been only five feet away from a determined assassin.

Their stay with the lovely hostess Ann ended and they set off on the return drive to London. Their route took them down the west coast through beautiful lush countryside and brought them that first night to Blackpool, a coastal holiday town. Many private houses were set up to rent rooms by the day or week, and Bob and Margaret found one for a night's stay. They had quite a surprise after being in the room for a while when the lights went out. Upon enquiry, they learned that electrical power was metered. Each room had a coin-operated meter and it had to be fed a shilling, much like our quarter, every two hours. The next day's drive brought them to London and an exhausting plane trip back to Toronto.

Several years later, when Bob and Margaret were almost forty, Margaret became pregnant after trying for ten years. They were blessed by the birth of their daughter Susanne. Margaret had a difficult time and was almost three days in labour. The doctors finally had to perform an emergency caesarean section to save the baby and the mother.

Several years before Susanne's birth, Bob was approached by his supervisor with the news that the company was considering him for promotion to store supervisor; after careful consideration, Bob concluded that his easy-going, open personality was not suited to oversee, manage, and perhaps discipline other managers, many older than himself, and consequently he declined the offer with thanks. He felt that this was a road to ulcer-causing, life-shortening pressure and was content to finish out his career managing the store.

Additionally, Bob and Margaret had other outside interests that were coming to fruition. With the help of a friend, an English fish-and-chipper from years back, they were opening a takeout seafood and fish-and-chip store on Kingston Road in Scarborough, about a mile east of the beer store.

Coordinating with his beer store shifts, Bob would go early to the King Neptune Fish & Chip store to receive deliveries, including fletches of huge Atlantic halibut. These were slightly frozen, four-inch-wide full cuts of the fish—fins, skin, and all. One section weighed about twenty pounds and Bob would then cut the fletch into thin two-ounce squares and fill plastic tubs enough for the day. If you cut too much too far ahead, the fish would lose juice and, consequently, flavour.

Margaret would arrive later and turn on the deep fryers and get the store ready for the day's business. When the orders started coming in, she would lift a piece of fish in one hand, lay it one side at a time in a tub of flour laced with MSG, then dip it into another tub of special batter. She then dropped it into the deep fryer and, after turning it over once, lifted it out, shook it well, and deposited it under the heat lamps. She cooked continually to keep ahead of the hungry customers, not just halibut but many different kinds of fish, as well as shrimp, scallops, and chicken.

She hired several teenage schoolboys to work part-time, including two of their friend Harold Maitland's boys, Bobby and Roy. Besides taking phone orders and bringing whatever Margaret needed to fill the orders, these boys cooked French fries in another deep fryer, two baskets at a time. When ready, they would lift them out, shake them vigorously and suspend them over the deep fryer to drain completely while the next two baskets cooked. The less grease in the end product, the better. Margaret had a very efficient system, with, the boys wrapping and filling orders as she served the product and worked the cash register. Bobby and Roy said in later years that they enjoyed working with Margaret. She taught them about a work ethic and good business practice, which stood them in good stead for the rest of their lives.

Ever since his early teenage years, Bob had enjoyed alcohol. It was only occasional—really minimal at first—but as the years rolled by, alcohol became more central to his life. It was eventually involved in every activity—playing golf, social activities, parties etc., and eventually he even drank in the beer store.

Bob became very good friends with two other beer store managers, Don Cufaro and Terry Field. They would go downtown together after work for dinner and drinks. They all enjoyed golf and would play together, of course with booze in the golf bag. More about this later.

Agnes Mary in 1970, age 45

Chapter Ten

BY 1973, WE FIND FRED AND AGNES MARY WITH FOUR of their six children—Rick, Gerald, and Jennifer, with Jannette in the basement apartment—safely ensconced in their rented house on Church Street in Vancouver. Janette, twenty-one and blessed with a lovely little girl named Vanessa, now two years old, is successfully on course to achieve a university degree.

Rick, their eldest son, was a talented enough hockey player for the NHL, although injuries at the semi-pro level sadly prevented that dream from becoming a reality. At age fifteen, Rick was captivated by a girl at school from the French islands of Saint-Pierre-et-Miquelon, situated just off Canada's east coast. Rick and Dominique were close friends for six years, marrying when Rick was twenty-one. After driving bus in Vancouver for fifteen years, Rick resigned and he and Dominique opened a computer sales and repair shop on Fourth Avenue. Five years later, the store next door became vacant; after renovations, they opened a coffee shop. This was the fulfillment of a dream Rick had for many years.

At thirteen, Gerald loved acting in school but he didn't show much interest in other, seemingly less important aspects of school like reading, writing, and arithmetic. In fact, galvanizing him to develop these scholastic talents required the stimulating presence of the one who ultimately became his wife, the lovely Robin, who helped propel him into a very successful business career.

Eight-year-old Jennifer found a new little sister in her niece Vanessa living downstairs. They were always in each other's house and became very close. This friendship remains to this day, even though their paths don't often cross due to the busyness of separate married lives.

Fred's two daughters by his first marriage, Beverly and Brenda, have been grown up and married since the Thompson days. Beverly has three boys and Brenda has a boy and a girl, so the Martin clan is growing. However, we haven't seen the end of their productivity. Stay tuned.

By 1980, Fred and Agnes Mary were forced to move three times, each time because the owners of their rental decided to sell the house. Beginning to feel that they should again become property owners, they bought a fixer-upper on Queens Street. Before very long, Fred was up to his armpits in renovations. Because of Fred's creative skills, the end result was a house so beautiful that Agnes Mary fell in love with it.

"This is it," she said. "I'll never move again."

Well, perhaps sometimes we had better be careful what we say.

Soon after this, Jannette began to attend church again. When she was just a young girl of thirteen, she had attended a Baptist church in Saskatoon with a girlfriend and prayed to receive Jesus Christ as her Lord and Saviour, but she did not follow up and moved away. However, God planted a seed in Janette, and through her the whole family subsequently came to God. As a mature adult, she returned to church and experienced a renewal of her faith. She attended church with eight-year-old Vanessa, and one day Vanessa asked her grandma why she didn't go to church with them. As Agnes Mary expressed later, "How can you say no to a sweet little granddaughter?"

Her visit to church was momentous. At the end of the service, Mary Agnes felt propelled to the front in response to the altar call. She was wonderfully born again that Sunday and was baptized in the Holy Spirit. Later at home, worshiping God in bed, she of course worshiped in the only language she knew—English— but could hear herself speaking out the words of another language she could not understand.

The story behind this event is recorded in the Bible, in Mark 16:17. Jesus appeared to His disciples after His crucifixion and told them that one of the signs which would follow them who believe in His name is that they would speak with new tongues. Later, in 1 Corinthians 12:7, the Apostle Paul explains that *"the manifestation of the Spirit is given to every man to profit withal,"* and in 12:10, one of the gifts listed is tongues. Lastly, in Acts 1:4–5, Jesus appeared to His apostles after His crucifixion and commanded that they should wait for God's promise of Holy Spirit baptism. In a wonderful extension of that promise, Jesus said, *"But ye shall receive power, after that the Holy Ghost [Spirit] is come upon you…"* (Acts 1:8) At this juncture, you might well ask, "The power for what?" He answers that question in the same verse: *"…and ye shall be witnesses unto me…"*

So we must conclude that God wishes primarily to empower Christians by His Holy Spirit to enable them to share the good news that the Saviour of the whole world, Jesus Christ, seated at the right hand of God the Father, has his arms wide open to welcome and receive every repentant seeker.

Agnes Mary became a force to be reckoned with as she enthusiastically shared her good news with all and sundry, but particularly with her family, beginning with Rick, who resisted somewhat until he witnessed a young girl walk into the path of a truck. He was undone by witnessing that life snuffed out in an instant, and the next night, he read a Christian pamphlet from Glad Tidings Church left on his bus. The pamphlet asked Rick if he knew where his soul would be immediately after he died, and that did it. Rick came weeping into God's kingdom.

All of Agnes Mary's family successively accepted Jesus as their Saviour soon after.

Chapter Eleven

WE FIND BOB AND MARGARET BOARDING WITH her sister Kay and brother-in-law Jim while they search for another place to live after selling their house prematurely. Bob is managing the beer store on Kingston Road in Scarborough as he and Margaret keep busy with the fish-and-chip store. Now in his early forties, Bob has developed a secret desire to own a farm out of town where they can be self-sufficient, maybe raise a cow and chickens, and grow their own food. After consultation with Margaret, they start searching.

Their search settled on a one-hundred-acre farm about forty miles northeast of Scarborough.

Bill, a burly Irishman, owned the farm with his wife, Fay. Bill was an auctioneer as well, and over the course of a year—that's how long the dickering and negotiating took—Bob and Margaret became friends with them. The long and short of it is, they bought the farm. After a few months, this green city family found themselves living on a farm and overseeing one hundred acres of badly fenced land. Over half of it was tillable, but about three acres was an open treed lot just northwest of the house. There were ten acres of hay and another ten of pasture. Looking east from the farm, the land sloped down over the next few farms in the middle distance and then gradually rose again to the far distant horizon. All of the fields were laid out in a vast checkerboard pattern of the loveliest shades of green. One could lie on the grass for hours drinking in God's beautiful creation.

Two large barns formed an L on two sides of an enclosed barnyard behind the large back lawn, east of the house. A long rickety shed stood on the north side of the same lawn and an excellent, spacious hen house was situated in the south east, next to the barnyard. A lovely kitchen garden at the front of the house faced west, overlooking the long lane leading down to a county concession road that fronted the property. That long lane became a headache later when the winter snows blew in, but in the euphoria of the moment, nothing could snow on their parade.

Bob and Margaret, with Susanne now eight and granddaughter Karen only four, were comfortably moved in. Their daughter Donna, Karen's mother, worked in Toronto. It was a good time for all. They enjoyed getting to know the neighbouring farmers, particularly the Goulds, a transplanted French Canadian family with a two-hundred-acre spread bordering on their north side. Dan Guild owned the equipment for planting and harvesting corn and grain, and was a great help to Bob as he got started in farming.

Bob eventually contracted with a livestock dealer to buy forty head of Hereford heifers from western Canada. One day when Bob was at work in Scarborough, a huge cattle truck backed up the farm lane unannounced and unloaded forty wild and woolly free-range heifers into the enclosed barnyard. Unfortunately, the corn was coming off and blowing into the recently built ground silo. When that clattering blower started to blow in the next load of chopped-up corn, stalks and all, the spooky cows broke through the fence and headed south to mix with a neighbouring farmer's cattle. They had quite a time cutting out those heifers and driving them back up to Bob's barnyard. In fact, three of the heifers could not be separated and Bob and the farmer agreed on a price to just leave them there.

With a borrowed Hereford bull named Ferdinand, Bob started a calf operation. The bull was owned by another neighbour, and the heifers enjoyed Ferdinand's company for a year while all Bob had to do was board him. He was a very contented and happy bull. They bought a horse for Susanne, a gelding called Blaze, and a potbellied pony called Sam for Karen to complete the family.

One very early fall morning, Bob was in a second floor bedroom, dressing for a trip to the beer store in Scarborough, when he glanced out the window overlooking the freshly harvested corn field. He saw, in the half-light, a skittish deer feeding on corn scraps.

So softly, morning sunrise flows o'er nearest ridge,
like molten honey inundating waiting fields below,
where creatures of the earth lie waiting for renewal,
while at forest's edge, a mother doe

so nervously will slowly venture out
from forest shelter onto farmer's furthest field,
at slightest sound, she skittishly peers all about,
where yesterday they harvested a bumper yield.

But then to hungrily begin her feeding,
she jumps at every sound,
then resumes so nervous, heeding.
A waiting week-old fawn makes
huge demands that must be met,
her milk must come, it's in God's hands.

Of all this fallen grain,
she must eat her fill,
while in sun-dappled forest glade,
her spotted fawn lies still.

Suddenly a farm door slams...
coiled spring legs releasing strong
and in a bound or two,
too rapid to believe, she's gone.

This mother doe returns to her fawn
who lies so still until at mom's behest,
she'll leap and fly, responding to her mom,
cause Mom knows best,
no asking why.

Deep in woods to rest,
to nurse on hidden forest lawn.
Yet another day, transpiring in a way,
that we can only guess,
for creatures of this world unseen,
who God will bless.
So as setting sun bespeaks day's end,
God also blesses you and me,
my poetry loving friend.

Bob contracted with Dan to plant and harvest oats and barley, as well as corn. One of the barns had a large granary inside and all the barley and oats were blown into those granaries at harvest time.

The corn was another story. With Dan and his equipment greatly assisting, they dug post holes around three sides of the perimeter. Using trees from Dan's woodlot and purchased plywood, they erected a ground silo into which the chopped-up corn could be blown. The open end of the ground silo faced into the barnyard, where all winter the heifers could feed from the corn through a strong slatted gate. This arrangement was great in theory, but in fact the thick top layer of corn would freeze and act like a roof as the cows undercut it. After Bob drove home from Scarborough on a few cold winter nights and walked up the long unploughed lane, he would have to climb on top of the frozen corn with a pickaxe and chop off the frozen overhang.

However, they got through that first winter. When spring arrived, so did a whole crop of beautiful white-faced Herford calves. The original forty calf heifers had been a little on the small side, and some had trouble calving. Bob spent many hours in the barn stalls with heifers on their sides, trying to calve, while he sat with feet braced against their butts. The calf's two feet would be sticking out, and because they were too slippery to hold onto, Bob would tie a double length of binder twine around them and coordinate his pull with her push, until finally a calf would slide out to add to the growing herd.

Margaret and Bob drove the forty miles back and forth to Scarborough every workday until they sold the fish-and-chip business two years later. After that, for three years Bob travelled alone, all the while drinking in the beer store, drinking in the barns, and drinking in the car while driving home some nights. It's only by the mercy and grace of God that disaster was averted.

Not infrequently, Bob would get a phone call at the beer store from Margaret, reporting that the cows had escaped through the fence somewhere. Margaret and the kids would have to find them and try bringing them back onto their property before they got into a neighbour's corn field. Bob would return as soon as possible to help and repair the fence for the umpteenth time.

Bob contracted with Dan to cut and bale the hayfield. The whole family would drive an old pickup truck out onto the field and load it up with bales and pile them next to the barn, where, with an electric elevator borrowed from Dan, they loaded all the baled hay into the loft. One year, Bob invited his two beer store manager friends, Don and Terry, to bring their families up to the farm for the weekend, and they all helped load the hay into the barn.

Along with some of the Gould kids, Susanne and Karen played for hours up in the hayloft, building forts and tunnels and hidden rooms in the baled hay. Bob thought there might have been a little adolescent kissing going on up there sometimes, but who knows?

Their first spring on the farm, Bob bought fifty unsexed chicks, both White Rock and Barred Rock, to raise for the freezer. It was necessary to clean out the old henhouse first and buy some automatic feeders and water bowls, along with heat lamps. Before long, the chicks were growing nicely. After they were half-grown, Bob noticed one of the hens terribly injured.

It turned out that she was being cannibalized by the others because their feed lacked enough protein. On Dan's advice, Bob bought soy beans which Dan ground and mixed that summer from Bob's own barley and oats. One unexpected benefit is that because half of them were hens, the family had a surplus of eggs which they enjoyed and shared with friends.

When the chickens were fully grown in late fall, everyone joined in to catch them and put them into crates, loading them onto the old pickup. Bob took them to a local company which plucked, cleaned, and bagged them for a small fee. The largest bird was fourteen pounds dressed, and they were the juiciest, tastiest chickens any of the family had ever tasted. Most of them were ultimately shared with family and friends, much to their delight.

As it seems all things must, this idyllic interlude in their lives after five years. The farm was sold and everything auctioned off. Bill officiated as the auctioneer. Everything came under the hammer— cows, calves, farm equipment, hay, grain, everything. Margaret and the girls made coffee, hamburgers, and hot dogs and sold them out the kitchen window. It was a well-advertised farm sale and many people attended from all around the district. It turned out to be quite an exciting and festive time for the family, but ultimately a sad reflective time as well.

A dramatic new chapter was about to begin with the end of the farm and the move to their new home, a lovely two-level cedar house on the shore of Lake Scugog, across from Port Perry,. The house had a walkout from the lower level to the dock, where very soon they would have a boat. This was two miles west of the farm. Although a little closer, it was still almost forty miles to Bob's work in Scarborough.

Margaret's mom and dad, who wintered in Florida, came to stay with them for two years in the summer months and occupied the lower suite. They were good company for her, since Bob was in the city more and more, or so it seemed to Margaret.

After their second summer with Bob and Margaret, her folks went once more to Florida for the winter. While down there, Margaret's dad died from a sudden heart attack. Her mother returned to live with her eldest son, Ray, and his family at Wasaga Beach, Ontario.

Agnes Mary on shopping trip
in Coquitlam in 1975 at age 50

Chapter Twelve

IN 1978, AGNES MARY ENTERED INTO A NEW AND exciting experience as a born-again Christian. She was enjoying a whole new church experience at Glad Tidings.

O'er her brief span of living,
while adventuring through life,
consume years in this vale of tears,
self-serving, oh so rife.

How limited, mortality,
how inward looking, vain,
how centred solely on oneself,
to ignorance sustain.

But thus goes man, without God's plan,
so blindly on his way,
oblivious to the truth God knew,
would make him free today.

Won't even try, but time went by,
quite self-sufficiently,
past halfway to the end, my friend,
Christ liberated me.

But God requires, 'fore time expires,
we take a step of faith,
one little step, it wasn't much,
then all my sins, erased.

Since then, life's had meaning,
it's no longer only me,
the same for you, you'll find it's true,
just take that step, you'll see.

She loved the unrestrained worship and all the busy activities. She joined the ladies prayer group and was part of other organized church ministries while Fred, an Anglican through and through, attended Glad Tidings only infrequently. He was, however, delighted to cook up a barbeque almost every summer Sunday when Agnes Mary invited people from church over to their house. She was content knowing that he was a devout believer in Jesus Christ as they all had a great time singing and praising God in the backyard. Occasionally some of the surrounding neighbours would sit out in their own yards and enjoy the singalong.

Their son Rick, after attending and participating with the youth, was on fire for Jesus. Along with his wife Dominique, he became a youth pastor for six years at another church, Victory Christian Centre.

Her younger son Gerald, along with his wife Robin, came to some special services although they didn't attend Glad Tidings regularly. They attended one such service when the baptism in the Holy Spirit was being ministered. They were both filled with laughter and tears of joy as they were baptized together and experienced a renewed enthusiasm for working in their church. For many years since, they've headed up an annual Christian retreat where people are born again and others experience renewal of faith.

Fred and Agnes Mary's youngest daughter, Jennifer, met a young man at Glad Tidings when she was eighteen, and he was to become her husband. Though Agnes Mary was not at all impressed by Kevin's appearance, Jennifer intuitively saw the diamond lurking behind his exterior, impatiently waiting to bust out. Kevin had been in the trucking business for himself and prospered until skyrocketing interest rates drove him out of business. When he met Jennifer, he was, as we used to say, on his uppers, living with his dog Tuka. He was down to his last box of cornflakes. Meeting Jennifer was turnaround for Kevin, the son of a retired pastor. Kevin found a wonderful job with a company that manufactures and installs cabinets in large builds, including high-rise condos, and before long he was promoted to installation supervisor.

Kevin and Jennifer served as youth pastors at Glad Tidings Church for ten years. They attended Bible College as well, where he earned a Master's degree. A little later, their second son Daniel met a lovely young lady. Together, they began attending Sunshine Hills Foursquare Church, where her dad, Tom, was head pastor. Daniel invited his whole family to church with him and they enjoyed it so much that they made it their home church. After Kevin became known to Pastor Tom, he was invited to become assistant pastor, an office he continues to hold to this day. He juggles what would ordinarily be two full-time careers with Jennifer's assistance, and she holds a full-time job as well. All the while, they succeeded in raising four outstanding young sons who are all serving the Lord.

Returning to that fixer-upper on Queens Street, the one Fred so wonderfully renovated, Agnes Mary was comfortably settled in and vowing never to move again. This was in 1980, and they once more began to prosper. Fred had a wonderful job with the Coast Guard, monitoring marine traffic on the west coast. Agnes Mary, after several brief office jobs, secured a position at the University of British Columbia as private secretary to professors at the Faculty of Law. Family life finally proceeded at a more normal rate, with the kids growing up, marrying, and moving out. Fred and Agnes Mary looked forward to an empty nest, and soon, a peaceful retirement.

With Fred's 1991 retirement date looming on the horizon, he had what he thought was a great idea: they had just a small mortgage and Fred wanted to be free of debt when he retired.

"Let's sell the house and look for a place a little ways out of town," he said. "We could buy a house mortgage-free in a less expensive neighbourhood.

Agnes Mary was adamantly opposed to the idea, and every time a real estate sign went up on the front lawn, she promptly pulled it down and hid it out back. This stalemate was unproductive, and certainly unchristian. One day, when Agnes Mary was praying and asking God to show Fred that they should stay, she distinctly heard that still, small voice in her heart suggest that, though God promised to give her the desires of her heart, that promise was for Fred also. Recognizing that she must relent, all heartfelt opposition melted away. When Fred came home that night, she told a very surprised husband that she now wanted to sell and move out of town with him.

With all barriers removed, Fred made arrangements to search real estate sales in Chilliwack, a community they had both admired when passing through in the past. Fred was by now retired and their last child was married and moved out. They spent several days in Chilliwack searching for just the right house at just the right price. They were becoming discouraged by the time they drove to the last listing for the day and found just what they had been looking for: a large quarter-acre lot with a beautifully appointed three-bedroom frame home with a full basement.

Chapter Thirteen

BOB'S LIFE WITH MARGARET AND SUSANNE IN THE house on the lake now settled into the daily routine of work, travelling back and forth to Scarborough, and visiting Donna, who was living in Queensville with her granddaughter Karen, her live-in friend Bill Bray, and Bill's four-year-old son Matthew. Bill, through a spiritual experience at his young wife's deathbed, recently became a new Christian. He and Donna married and started attending church with the two kids. Over time, they grew together as Christians and tried getting Bob and Margaret to go to church with them. Bob would have none of it. He said that he was glad for them, but they should make sure to have a bottle of rum in the house when he came to visit.

Problems, though, were simmering at home, instigated by Bob's increasing absence. Bob often joined his friends Don and Terry after work for evenings of dinner and drinks downtown, driving home in the wee hours. Although Margaret gently complained, Bob felt entitled to enjoy this diversion from life's intense demands, what with managerial responsibilities and a forty-mile drive twice a day. Sadly, they were growing apart as Margaret gradually withdrew. Their relationship degenerated to the point where they no longer spoke to each other anymore.

Bob began to feel that his marriage was ending. This was bitter and sad for him, for he had been proud of his successful marriage while both his sister's and brother's marriages had ended in divorce. Margaret's personality was such that she kept everything inside and wouldn't discuss her inner feelings.

One morning, very early, Bob couldn't sleep and found himself seated in the living room looking out over the lake through the large picture window. He was wrestling with these problems and finally concluded that his marriage was finished. He was heartbroken and felt like a failure, but he decided that it was time to break up his home and end the marriage.

Right at that moment, he noticed the Bible that Bill and Donna had recently left on the table.

What the heck is this thing all about? he thought. He picked it up, cracked it open somewhere near the middle, and read the first verse his eye fell upon.

Bob was suddenly bathed in a sweet, intense love. A delightfully euphoric, glorious joy filled his whole being and a distinct inner voice said, "Show more interest in your home and family." This was not an audible voice but was as clear as if it had been cast in stone and brightly illuminated.

Bob knew, as all must know unmistakably when God speaks, that it was God. In a daze, he went into the kitchen and thought to make coffee. He fell on his knees to the kitchen floor and wept copiously, pouring out contrition and remorse. He didn't know how long he stayed there, but when he arose he was cleansed by God's Holy Spirit, a brand new man.

What a glorious bursting forth of light
What a transformation to daylight from night
What a renewal, what a delight
Everything lovely and shiny and bright,
for God is Love.

While all of this was transpiring in the kitchen, while the very God of all glory visited their house, Margaret remained asleep in the bedroom, totally oblivious to the fact that her whole world was changing most dramatically. She must have thought Bob was drinking extra early that day when her happy husband woke her up and asked what she needed him to do around the house.

Bob explained to a very bewildered Margaret all that had happened while she slept. He lovingly reassured her and they were eternally reconciled. Margaret's nature was to be quiet and reserved, but she fell right into step with Bob as they set out to find a local church and set their lives on track with God. When they had first married, Margaret prayed every night before bed, but Bob did not and gradually she lost the habit. Bob became convinced that God had watched over her throughout their marriage. He later said that he'd always thought their marriage problems were Margaret's fault, but God didn't reprimand her, only him. Bob said, though, that even God's reprimand was sweet.

Bill and Donna had been praying for them for months. You can just imagine Donna's joy when Bob phoned her from the beer store later that day with the good news. It isn't every day that we get such an answer from God. She and Bill were overjoyed.

Bob and Margaret looked for a church in Port Perry and were attracted to a quaint wooden church. Denomination meant nothing to them, but this one happened to be Pentecostal and was co-pastored by two unmarried lady ministers, Sister Iris McLean and Sister Ruby Batten. They were delighted to welcome a new family into their small church and invested much time and energy grounding them in the way of salvation, water baptism, and Bible teaching. Bob and Margaret expressed thanks to God for leading them to that church, under the wing of these two ladies at this crucial beginning of their Christian walk.

Bob continued as beer store manager for the next five years, and by the grace of God he never had another alcoholic drink, with one exception. This occurred soon after his conversion, when he had lunch at a Greek restaurant next to the beer store. It was just before Christmas and he was friends with the proprietor, having hired his young son part-time at the beer store. Bob ordered lunch with coffee and soon the waitress brought a Coca-Cola to the table—by mistake, Bob thought. Since he was thirsty, he tossed back about half of the glass and was shocked to realize that it was rum and coke. He looked up to see the proprietor grinning at him through the kitchen serving window and mouthing "Merry Christmas." Bob shrugged, saluted with the glass, and finished the rest in one gulp. Because God had delivered him from alcohol, and because he was innocent of intent, the drink had no lasting effect on him and he never had another alcoholic drink after that. It has now been thirty five years.

Because Bob personally met with God that day at home, he was able with authority the good news that Jesus Christ is alive and loves them. He told all his friends at Brewers Warehousing Company, both those who worked in his store and with his manager friends. With great joy, he shared the revelation with his extended family and with personal friends and acquaintances.

After a few years of Bible study and church attendance, at his son-in-law's invitation, he visited *100 Huntley Street*'s Christian television studio and joined with the other telephone volunteers during the one-hour daily telecast. His son-in-law, Bill Bray, had been the show's director since the ministry's inception; he continues to this day as a producer.

Bob felt increasingly hypocritical. He was praying fervently for his young teenage daughter Susanne, that God would protect her from sin, drugs, and alcohol, while at the same time he was intimately involved in supplying alcohol to other teenagers as a beer store manager. He talked with Margaret about resigning and naturally met with a great deal of resistance. One Friday, when he felt he could continue no longer, he wrote a letter of resignation, slipped it in the large envelope with his month-end reports, and drove home to break the news to Margaret.

Well, this opened up a hornet's nest of recrimination, tears, and defeat with Margaret all Saturday night and all day Sunday. He couldn't even sleep Sunday night. He realized that he had done the wrong thing by forcing this on her without her agreement. After being up all night, he drove down to head office early enough to intercept the courier Monday morning. He identified himself to the night watchman, then entered before staff arrived. Over one hundred envelopes were lying on the huge boardroom table. After a frantic search, he found his envelope, extracted his letter of resignation, and beat it out of there with a great sigh of relief. When he returned home that night, Margaret forgave him and all was well again.

But of course, his problem was by no means resolved. He got back into the old routine and life resumed its same old course. Bob couldn't pray for Susanne with any conviction and felt that his Christian walk was being compromised. He and Margaret had many long talks and prayers together about this, until the season arrived when his pension was about to be instituted. Bob felt that he couldn't allow himself to be supported for life by the sale of beer, and finally Margaret came into agreement, bless her heart. With a month left until his pension was set, Bob made an appointment to see the superintendent of stores at head office.

Bob was ushered into Fred's office, and with very little preamble he dropped his bombshell. Fred was puzzled and unable to understand. He asked Bob if they as a company had done anything to cause this, which gave Bob an opportunity to share how Jesus had changed his life. He reassured Fred that the company had always been very good to him, but that he must now embark on a new path in life. Bob asked Fred if he would like to have the same experience, and Fred said that he was okay; his good deeds would outweigh his bad deeds. Bob explained that works would not save him, that only a relationship with Jesus could do that.

They parted on that note, and Bob's severance pay and documents were subsequently prepared and delivered. Bob never went back to the beer store.

An interesting but very sad side note: a few weeks later, Fred had a brain aneurism and never regained consciousness. Bob tried to see him in the hospital but could not, since only family was allowed. Bob hoped that his witness to Fred had been God-ordained and that Fred was with Jesus in heaven.

As Bob drove away from head office the day he resigned, after twenty-seven years of the world's security, he was attacked by severe doubts and despair. As he drove up the Don Valley Parkway, he detoured in desperation to his friend Harold Maitland's house. He just had to have some consolation.

When Bob explained the situation to Harold, he immediately came up with some suggestions for how Bob could get his job back. This only deepened Bob's anguish. He rushed out, drove home, and closeted himself with his Bible. He just had to hear from God.

Bob was in anguish. Had he been too hasty? Was God even aware of him, and if so, what was he doing? Where was God in all this? He had to know. He poured over his Bible in desperation.

Help me, Lord, he prayed. *I'm lost without You.*

Then, eureka, he found it! A word from God just for him. It jumped off the page and peace filled his heart as he read and reread the comforting words of Isaiah 54:7–8:

> *For a small moment have I forsaken thee; but with great mercies will I gather thee. In a little wrath I hid my face from thee for a moment; but with everlasting kindness will I have mercy on thee, saith the Lord thy Redeemer.*

What wonderful words. The Lord had emphasized the brevity of his reprimand with the words "small moment," "little wrath," and "for a moment."

Agnes Mary at Christian
women's retreat in 1985, age 60

Chapter Fourteen

FOR THE NEXT FIFTEEN YEARS, FRED AND AGNES MARY lived an idyllic existence in Chilliwack. Agnes Mary, who loved gardening, was in her glory planting trees and corn and potatoes and carrots and on and on. She looked forward every spring to a new garden and felt positively poetic about it, singing quietly in her heart.

Ah, Spring! The barren earth seems locked in death,
but the miracle of life is stirring, striving upward,
pressing, surging, commanding
that first promised resurrection breath,
of wind and sun, the warm sustaining rain's begun,
to melt confining ice and snow,
those frozen prisons down below,
releasing Spring's eternal glory, lusting for the sun.

Life's essence surging, bursting up, from every root,
each fruit tree thirsty,
budding out her lovely blossoms all about,
the portent of a harvest soon, of life sustaining fruit.
No thought of Winter's imminence, each lovely tree;
no anticipating, no regretting,
no remembering, no forgetting,
let's blossom with them in this moment, you and me.

Fred's mind, on the other hand, was of a more practical bent. He focused on the need for lots of water to keep her garden flourishing.

This great big earth as it floats in the sky,
no change since creation we cannot deny,
all the moisture and water originally there
doesn't leave our closed system, can't go anywhere,
just circulates round from the earth to the sky
then back to the earth where you're wondering why
when you stop for a drink from a watering can,
that water's been here since creation began,
you're just part of the system so then when you go
to the bathroom and flush and it goes down below
to be mixed in with all of the water on earth
and made perfectly pure as it was at the birth
of our planet when God with creation's great plan
put it all here in place provide water for man
and for all of the plants and the trees that grow
by transpiration, condensation up the water must go,

the wind from the ocean that blows o'er the land
circulating the moisture exactly as planned
as it forms into clouds away up high
where it cools and then water can fall from the sky
back down to earth where we all get a drink,
now I've come to the end of my story I think,
if this sentence grows longer it'll scare me to death
so I just have to stop 'cause I've run out of breath.

Fred also loved to tinker and was now in tinker heaven, spending almost four years to completely rebuild an older burned-out house trailer. He stripped it right down to the frame and made it like new again. He moved it to a lot on Lake Skaha in Penticton, where the whole family enjoyed summer holidays for many years and where it continues to give others pleasure to this very day.

The wheel of life must continue to turn,
inexorably moving us on.
Warmth of summer sadly past,
evenings cool at sun's descent,
heads with silver hues now cast,
I wonder where the summer went.

Those endless, languid days replete,
with cooling draughts in leafy shade,
sweet children, innocently meet,
where golden bonds for life were made.

Sun kissed summers long before,
as far as our young minds could see,
stretched endless on, those days of yore,
to love forever, he and thee.

In spring when all is flush with life,
where beauty, strength, life's energy
flow up through growing saplings rife,
with faith to live eternally.

But as the wheel of life revolves,
life's essence slowly slips away,
our glory, back to earth evolves,
new saplings rising, take the day.

To grow in strength and majesty,
to overtake their waning sires
who crumble now for all to see,
as strength depletes, as life expires.

But leave us not be too undone,
for life is rising out of death,
the old must pass, the new must come,
to give God praise with every breath.

With joyous heart, we now observe,
this new life rise to our content,
God's bounty, more than we deserve,
time swiftly flies, where summer went.

In 2006, after this fifteen-year period in their lives, time for Fred flew away for good when he suddenly passed away from prostate cancer, leaving Agnes Mary to face life alone. The house in Chilliwack that was once such a blessing now held too many memories. It became too much for her to continue living there alone, so after consulting with her family, it was decided that she would live with her daughter Jennifer. Very reluctantly, the source of her pride and joy was listed on the real estate market and she painfully relinquished the garden she loved so much.

Kevin and Jennifer were at that time looking for a larger house in Surrey and now planned to look for one with a separate, self-contained apartment for Grandma.

Her house in Chilliwack sold quickly and Agnes Mary, on her own, advertised and successfully sold almost everything they owned—truck, car, trailer, and most of the household furnishings.

Her house-hunting daughter and son-in-law now had a deadline and the hunt became feverish. At the eleventh hour, success! After Kevin did some major remodelling, a nice two-bedroom, ground-level apartment was ready for Agnes Mary to move right in. Much to her delight, there was a lovely enclosed garden right outside her back door. She was happy again, with a place to plant her favourite flowers, daisies, and watch the bees pollinating all day.

She lingers now with head so grey,
where plots of happy daisies play.
They sprightly dance and look about,
communicating there without

the slightest voice to scarce suggest,
response to bumble bee's request
to openly access sweet treasure,
preserved by daisy's all together

deep within their virgin hearts,
where bees intrude in fits and starts,
to probe and search for treasure deep,
so tirelessly, no time for sleep,

for hungry hive at home awaits
the stream of bees through open gates,
as endlessly their treasure bring,
then ceaselessly on golden wing,

depart again for treasure trove,
as over countryside they rove,
working tirelessly for man,
to sweeten us, a lovely plan.

While daisies, after giving all,
must perish with approaching fall.
This whole arrangement's just for us,
they sacrifice without a fuss.

The daisies beautify her place,
then to the bees their treasure grace.
Sweet honey trove her happy fate,
while all she has to do is wait.

Now, where did those bees hide all that honey?

*Bob McCluskey seeking God
in Bible study in 1983, age 57*

*Bob McCluskey joined Faith Center Church in
Toronto, becoming board chair under
Doctor Winston Nunes, pictured center...Silly hats
worn by Stan Buxton (Treasurer) and Bob McCluskey
...Three embarrassed wives attended*

Chapter Fifteen

BOB AND MARGARET HAD THROWN THEMSELVES completely on God's provision when they agreed that he should resign. Now he had a lot more time to volunteer at *100 Huntley Street*, and he gave himself to helping out all he could. They had some savings and could survive for a while, but they were praying real hard for God to direct their next step.

The answer was not too long in coming. While at the TV studio one day, Bill introduced Bob to Graham Kerr, the famous television personality who at one time had a cooking show and had walked away from it through a series of circumstances when he and his wife and two children had all become Christians.

Graham was now on staff with a Christian missionary ministry called Youth With a Mission (YWAM) and was filling in at *100 Huntley Street* as host while David Mainse was away for two weeks. His life direction changed to honour God, just as Bob's had, although his sacrifice was much greater than Bob's.

Graham and Bob had lunch together. When Graham learned of the change in Bob's life, he very enthusiastically recommended that Bob should definitely consider joining YWAM for a six-month term. If you have ever seen one of his shows, you will know how very enthusiastic and persuasive he can be.

Bob and Margaret talked it over and felt that God was opening this door. They began negotiations with YWAM's Hawaii base to enroll in a program called Crossroads Discipleship Training School (Crossroads DTS). Although YWAM was a ministry designed for young people, this new DTS was for middle-aged or older people who were at a crossroads in their lives, as Bob and Margaret were. After a short period communicating back and forth, they were accepted as a family for that program and a place was made for Susanne to attend a school near the base.

This was the beginning of a very hectic time in their lives, for they now had to put their lovely lake home up for sale and arrange to store all of their furniture and belongings. Their home received an offer to buy, which they accepted, with a closing date the day before their flight for Hawaii. A last-minute glitch threatened to derail everything, but at the eleventh hour this was resolved. They stayed that last night with their daughter Donna, who took them to the airport the next day. Glory be, they were off for Hawaii.

Bob, Margaret, and Susanne will never forget their late evening arrival in Hawaii. They deplaned into a velvety soft tropical evening with the perfume of multitudes of flowers filling the night air. When they arrived at the YWAM base on the big island that evening, they were billeted in a modern high-rise hotel right on the ocean. Since the accommodations on the base were full, two floors of this hotel were reserved for YWAM. The hotel had a large outdoor swimming pool right on the edge of the ocean, surrounded by tropical foliage. When Margaret returned to the hotel each afternoon, the first thing she did was put on her bathing suit and spend a leisurely hour or two gently swimming up and down in the pool. A shuttle bus picked them up every morning and returned them every evening after dinner. All their meals were taken on the base in the main dining room; the food was healthy and adequate but Spartan. The menu was created compliments of Graham Kerr, who was designing healthy menus only from the resources available to third-world peoples.

Right in the base and on a high bluff overlooking the Pacific was a large, open-sided pavilion where they gathered every day for three months of teaching classes. What a place to spend the day! Soft, warm breezes came in under the roof through the wide open sides. They could gaze through tropical palm fronds down to the sparkling Pacific and listen to the lovely bird songs.

But hark! In quietness of thought
a trilling lyric sweet is caught
by listening ear tuned close to hear...
God's sweet soloist is near.
To worship, trembling heart emote
a paean of love from pulsing throat.
Feathered creature poet lauds,
fluffs to sleep as heaven applauds.
Survive the night, at morning light
bursting into joyful flight
to trumpet forth their praise on high
defiant... decorate the sky.
By God's design they pleasure bring
to eyes and ears of serf or king.
Their destiny to entertain,
men deafened to their sweet refrain.
But faithful, fulfill destiny,
next generation we will see
graduate from music class.
Some never to be heard... Alas!

Everybody on the base took turns one way or another to help out with daily tasks. Bob's task was to draw on the blackboard, with coloured chalk, a fancy menu rhyme depicting dinner. The only one he can now remember was when the base's fishing boat caught a shark. It went like this:

There's a wonderful tale that we'd like to relate,
'bout that fillet of shark that you find on your plate.
Our finny friend suffered a terrible fate,
he thought he'd be eating, instead he got ate;
and they did eat the shark and he was delicious.

When Bob first arrived, he found that he was attacked every morning for a week or so by a terrible fear. The thoughts would come crashing in on him: *You have no job. You have no home. You are not a minister. You are a nobody. You have no income. You will be destitute.* He would leap out of bed, get into the shower, turn it up full blast, and begin to yell out at the top of his voice who he was: "I am a child of God. I can do all things through Christ who strengthens me. I am the head and not the tail. If God be for me, who can be against me? God works all things together for good to them who love Christ Jesus, and that's who I am." Very quickly the panic would leave him and his peace was restored. After about a week, the attacks stopped.

Their first three months at YWAM were spent attending the scheduled teaching and ministry program, and for the second three months Bob attended the counselling school, the nucleus of what ultimately became an accredited university. Margaret volunteered to join the hospitality staff and was involved in looking after visiting teachers and ministers.

The YWAM base was located on the Kona coast of the big island, Hawaii. A red double-decker English-style bus travelled up and down the highway from the city of Kailua Kona to all the coastal hotels. The bus was free and was intended to bring tourist business into the city. Bob and Margaret would hop the bus into the city now and again to a restaurant situated right on the coast where they served a really great juicy hamburger, a tasty change from the base diet. The restaurant's open-walled dining room was suspended out over the Pacific, and on a warm, tropical night with the moonlight sparkling on the water through palm foliage, it was wonderful.

As their six-month stay in Hawaii came to an end, Bob and Margaret were again faced with the prospect of what to do, where to live. One evening in their hotel room, they decided to pray for guidance and kneeled down on either side of the bed. After praying, both quietly waited on God.

After what seemed like hours, but was probably only five minutes, Bob said that he had heard nothing. Margaret said that she had heard nothing either. Then she asked Bob if he thought Isaiah 16 meant anything, as this had come into her mind as she was waiting. Bob excitedly said, "Yes! Yes! That's an answer from God." He sat back on the bed, propped the Bible on his knees, and they proceeded to carefully study the whole chapter.

It took a while, but suddenly Bob could see some direction in Isaiah 16:2–4. He felt that God was directing them to provide a house where young unsaved girls could stay, young girls who were scattered and homeless, who had fled to the city of Toronto looking for some security and were vulnerable to be preyed upon for the sex trade.

Feeling now that they had a new purpose, though lacking any resources to finance such a beginning, they returned to Toronto and stayed with Donna and Bill. Bob returned to *100 Huntley Street* as a volunteer, and before long he was offered the paid position of head of the Security Counselling department. This entailed around-the-clock building security and manning the counselling phones with a staff of five or six volunteers.

Needing to be on their own, they leased an apartment in Scarborough and recovered their stored furniture. The superintendent of their building one day asked them if they would agree to be assistant superintendents, and a few months later, when the resident superintendents resigned hurriedly, Bob and Margaret were offered the full position and found that God had answered their prayers, blessing them exceedingly. The new apartment that went with this position provided an extra bedroom. Seeking to fulfill the mandate they felt God had given them, they looked for an opportunity to begin.

In his position at *100 Huntley Street*, Bob sometimes had occasion to minister to people who came to the studio door after hours and was able, on two separate occasions, to bring home young destitute girls to nurture and put on the right path. Margaret, of course, was in full agreement and together they worked to help these girls.

They were eventually able to reunite the first girl with her family, but the second girl was beyond their capacity to cope with. She was totally disobedient and uncooperative, and one day she quietly left of her own volition. After a few more false starts, they decided to just wait on God for His direction and put that dream on the shelf.

Chapter Sixteen

WHILE BOB AND MARGARET WERE ADVENTURING IN Ontario, Agnes Mary's life in British Columbia had come to an end, as far as she could tell. God, however, still had plans for her.

Agnes Mary was settling into her lovely new apartment at the home of Kevin and Jennifer and their four strapping sons. This, the perfect house, had to fit their budget, be located strategically, and have the bedrooms and bathrooms sufficient for themselves and four grown sons. And finally, but importantly, it had to pass Grandma's approval.

After Kevin renovated, decorated, and installed everything, including a new kitchen, Agnes Mary was delighted. This was, of course, a strange neighbourhood to her, so getting settled involved an extended period of exploration and trial-and-error shopping trips, which for a while meant frequent phone calls home.

"Kevin, help. Where am I?"

"Okay, Mom, just tell me what stores you see around you.

"Canadian Tire."

"Okay, just wait there and I'll be right over in two minutes."

Kevin would show up right away and lead Agnes Mary back home. But after a while, she knew her way around like a native and her kids could relax when she took the car out. However, she would not drive in the rain or snow—and never in the dark, even to this day.

And so her new life began. Everything from her old house was gone, including transportation, so she needed to get a new car for those shopping excursions. Her two boys, Rick and Gerald, put their heads together to select just the right car for her. They visited car showrooms, poured over advertisements, and checked specifications until finally they both agreed on the right car for Mom. Armed with absolute confidence in her two experts, Agnes Mary made her purchase and has enjoyed a great car experience ever since.

Living downstairs from her loving family, Agnes Mary only needed to cook if she felt like it. At about four or five in the afternoon, she would hear a knock at the door and Jennifer or Kevin, or even one of the boys, would come in and ask if she would like some of their dinner. The next question out of her mouth would be "Wadda ya got?" Her acceptance would depend on whether or not Kevin was cooking Mexican that night, which he sometimes did. They all loved Mexican food upstairs, but unfortunately Agnes Mary did not.

Kevin loved to cook and Jennifer loved to let him. Mexican was on the menu so much because the family travelled down to Mexico every other year to minister in homes and churches in a particular area where they had many friends. One year, the teenage son and daughter of their Mexican friends were hosted by Kevin and Jennifer for a week in Canada. They came to Surrey and were shown the city and the local sights. Sunshine Hills Church had the pleasure of getting a demonstration of authentic Mexican music and dancing by these two young people wearing striking costumes.

In Chapter Twelve, Agnes Mary's grandson Daniel was fatally smitten by a young lady, Elisia Gardner, whose parents Tom and Lottie were church pastors. Daniel came from a family of four boys and Elisia from a family of four girls. If they had just one more, they would equal the family of Tevye and Golde in *Fiddler on the Roof*. This does sound a little like a movie script or a romance novel, doesn't it? Iut it's real life, folks, and no, the four girls did not marry the four boys. C'mon, let's be real here! However, Elesia did eventually marry Daniel, and even one out of four ain't bad.

So we find two families eternally locked together in holy matrimony. All of Pastor Tom and Lottie's daughters were now married and all of Pastor Kevin and Jennifer's sons were unmarried, except their second son Daniel—at least up to this present time.

100 Huntley St. T.V. program,
from left to right host David Mainse,
Bob McCluskey next, Dynamic Arthur Blessitt who
carried a literal cross around the world for Christ
next and David's right hand man
Cal Bombay on right end.
Bob McCluskey headed 100 Huntley St. Security
Counselling Dept. and was on air guest with Arthur
Blessitt that day...Approx. year 1985, Bob aged 58

Chapter Seventeen

BOB AND MARGARET CONTINUED SUPERINTENDING the apartment building while Bob worked at *100 Huntley Street*. Their daughter Susanne now had two boys, Robert and Avery, with her husband Tony, but their marriage was suffering. Tony worked at General Motors in Oshawa and was doing drugs and drinking. Susanne prevailed on him to attend a church retreat and dedicate his life to God. This change was short-lived and the situation became intolerable. Susanne left Tony for the third and last time, then came to Bob and Margaret's apartment with the two boys. After a fruitless and emotional visit from Tony the next day to convince her to come back, he left.

Bill Bray, Donna's husband, was released from *100 Huntley Street* and the family moved to British

Columbia. Bill had visited B.C. earlier in his career as a TV director and fell in love with the province. This was his opportunity to relocate there.

Through their friendship with an upscale jeweller and goldsmith in Victoria, Bill and Donna were encouraged to start their own jewellery store, and before long Caring Jewellery and Gifts was open for business in the city of Duncan on Vancouver Island. They bought a lovely home on the city outskirts and were soon settled and on their way to live happily ever after.

When Donna learned of her sister's recent separation, she suggested that Susanne might enjoy moving out to B.C. to live with her and Bill. Susanne decided to do just that. With financial help from Mom and Dad, she and the two boys were soon on a plane to B.C.

After living with Bill and Donna for a while, Susanne met a young man from Shawnigan Lake, near Duncan, a new Christian. Love blossomed, and after her divorce was finalized David Jorgensen and Susanne were married. The boys now had a new father.

Bob and Margaret found themselves alone and without family just as *100 Huntley Street* was about to move into a new ministry home in Burlington, Ontario. The prospect of commuting the thirty miles from Scarborough to Burlington each day held no attraction for Bob. He and Margaret saw this as an opportunity to make another major change in their lives, and they took the plunge. Bob resigned from *100 Huntley Street* and from the board of Pastor Winston Nunes' church, Faith Temple, on Broadview Avenue in Toronto. He and Margaret also resigned from their position of building superintendent and proceeded to make arrangements for the trip out west.

They decided to make this a bit of an adventure and arranged with a moving company to load all of their belongings onto a moving van. This, of course, is a common enough occurrence, but to their surprise their car could be shipped the same way. With nothing to encumber them except their luggage, they bought a pair of one-way Via Rail tickets, Toronto to Vancouver, with a drawing room. They were on their way.

We used the word "adventure" in the previous paragraph very intentionally, because this cross-country journey turned out to include a series of delays and breakdowns that eventually brought them into Vancouver a day late and quite a few dollars short.

The difficulties began the first night out in Northern Ontario when the train could not proceed and had to come to a stop in the black of night out in the wilds. They had to back up, retracing the ground they had covered for many miles, and then take an alternate route. The next night, they couldn't get heat back to their sleeping car because the water supply was low and the steam heat had to be rationed.

On they travelled up over the head of the lakes past Port Arthur and Fort William (now amalgamated into Thunder Bay) and out onto the prairies. Navigating through the train to get to the dining car each day at meal times became part of the adventure. The space between cars was a moving, bouncing steel platform covered in ice which was crossed in very hazardous fashion, holding each other up and praying hard. The best that can be said is that the freezing air helped their appetites in preparation for dinner.

The next leg of their journey found them in the wee hours of the night, pulling into a suburban Winnipeg station. The sink in their drawing room would not work and the porter promised to have it repaired at the next stop.

The drawing room had a huge window, in front of which Bob and Margaret lay in bed at window height. They looked out on a freight platform, deserted except for a few workmen looking in as they stood under the platform lights. The men's warm breath billowed like clouds of steam in the frigid air as they talked. Next there came a knock on the door and two huge freezing workmen clothed in layers of canvas work clothes entered their drawing room. Now remember, this was not a spacious drawing room as you might have seen in a movie. No, this was a train, after all, and the very small room left only a narrow space to walk past the bed to get at the sink. Bob and Margaret lay there feeling quite exposed, clutching the covers up around their necks as these two ice-cold giants hovered over them banging and clanging with wrenches and torches an arm's length away from their heads. Eventually they got the water running again and left, leaving the cold behind them.

These events necessitated a further delay, and each time this occurred, on at least three or four occasions, they were compensated with a complimentary breakfast. They did appreciate the gesture, for what else could the train crew do? But one unfortunate aspect of all these delays was that they passed through the Rockies at night. This would have been the most spectacular part of the whole trip and they were sorely disappointed to have to sleep right through it. They hoped that one day they'd have another chance to see the Rockies first hand.

Chapter Eighteen

BEFORE JOINING PASTOR TOM AS ASSISTANT PASTOR at Sunshine Hills Foursquare Church, Kevin and Jennifer had been ordained youth pastors at Glad Tidings Church for about ten years. In 2007, in the natural course of things, Agnes Mary joined her family on Sundays and began to attend their new church. Before long she was invited to join what was called the mini-church, a Wednesday night meeting of mostly seniors from Sunshine Hills who gathered at the home of Jack and Margaret Neilson for fellowship, hymn singing, and Bible study. The informal gathering was headed by retired pastors Victor and Dorothy Gardner, the mom and dad of Pastor Tom Gardner.

Victor and Dorothy Gardner were both born in the United States. They met and married there, attended

Bible College there, and were ordained as pastors there by the Foursquare Church denomination. The first Foursquare Church was established in Los Angeles in 1927 by a Canadian woman, greatly anointed of God, called Sister Aimee Semple McPherson.

For its time, the church was enormous, seating over five thousand, and there eventually was a Bible college built on the same property.

This church was the nucleus of what ultimately became in 2000, mostly under the leadership of the founder's son, Rolf K. McPherson, a worldwide denomination of sixty thousand churches with a membership of over eight million in 144 countries. This enormous, vibrant growth happened in just a little over seventy years.

Victor and Dorothy Gardner were appointed as pastors to the Foursquare Church in Dover, Ohio in 1958 and left to assume duties in Burnaby, B.C. in 1974. During their sixteen-year tenure in Dover, they experienced a very busy time of church growth and oversaw the financing and creation of a large new church building, which they left without debt. Victor and Dorothy's two sons declared that they grew up there in a great environment, in what son Tom described as "white picket fence land."

Victor and Dorothy moved to Canada in response to the offer of a multi-tiered challenge from head office. They would be responsible simultaneously to fill the office of Western District supervisors, Bible college directors, and last but not least, local church pastors. My description here is in the plural, for it includes Dorothy for the very good reason that the job would have been impossible without her equally important contribution. Who knows? Maybe she was even more important, but don't tell Victor we said that.

In any event, that was all behind them as they rested on their oars and enjoyed a well-earned retirement. They kept their hands occupied heading up the seniors mini-church, but that wasn't work to them. That was just having fun with old friends.

Agnes Mary enjoyed Victor and Dorothy's ministry, as well as all her newfound friends at mini-church. For some time she had been driving herself to the Wednesday night meetings. However, because of her concern for night driving, Victor and Dorothy started picking her up and taking her home, as they lived in her area.

She was, however, beginning to feel somehow unfulfilled and felt the need for a closer friendship. It had been about four years since Fred gad died and the grieving period had been over for a while.

It's a strange thing that the human heart can faithfully love another for so many years, and even when that loved one is gone, the love they had does not end, but lasts forever in the spirit. A new relationship does not diminish that first love but enables the human heart to love once more, for God is love.

Chapter Nineteen

BOB AND MARGARET'S ARRIVAL IN B.C. BROUGHT A wonderful reunion time with the kids. A year earlier, they had financed the down-payment on a two-family house in Duncan where David and Susanne lived upstairs, temporarily renting out the lower suite in anticipation of Bob and Margaret's later arrival.

While living there, Bob and Margaret visited with Bob's nephew from the U.S., his sister Ethel's son Harold. Harold had successfully started up a business in the U.S. called All American Eyeglass Repair. He shared the details of the business with David and Susanne and encouraged them that they could make it work up in Canada as well. Soon David and Susanne started All Canadian Eyeglass Repair, helped by Harold's expertise and encouragement. This business venture necessitated a move down to Vancouver for the whole family, where they became well-established, David and Susanne in their townhouse in Surrey and Bob and Margaret in their townhouse in White Rock.

David and Susanne, with their three children—Robert, Avery, and Elizabeth—found a church they liked in Delta called Sunshine Hills Foursquare Church and they began to attend there. In due course, Bob and Margaret decided to try it out and were warmly welcomed by the people. Dorothy Gardner approached them and invited them to a Wednesday night house meeting of mostly church seniors. and before long they were attending there regularly as well.

After a year or two, Margaret took ill and was admitted to Peace Arch Hospital. She was placed in intensive care and, to the shock and despair of Bob and the whole family, she passed away.

Bob had previously purchased side-by-side burial plots in a small graveyard very near Susanne's house, and Margaret was buried there in the military section, since she had been in the Canadian Army during the Second World War. Pastors Victor and Tom officiated at the graveside ceremony (and they will do so again for Bob when Bob's time comes). As Bob expressed it, the pastors and many church friends were a great comfort and help at that time.

This was a very difficult time for Bob, for he loved Margaret very much and could not imagine life without

her. He found himself reviewing their life together and
remembering her sweetness.

How warmly recall as life's reaching the end,
those years long ago, you became my friend.
That first day together, remember it yet,
we were both apprehensive, I'll never forget,
How you sweetly, discreetly, surreptitiously,
stole my heart with that first kiss, deliciously.
You were always so tiny, so wonderfully sweet,
I was clumsy, left footed, tripped over my feet.
You danced like a dream, jitterbugged at the ball,
awkward and stiff, I was liable to fall.
Made plans for our life, just starting from scratch,
me on cloud nine, with my wonderful catch.
We faced life together, with never a fear,
of opportunity's door, when it would appear.
You always encouraged, you never held back,
with every new venture, you kept me on track.
Those fifty four years, you were always the same,
always stylish, petite, you carried my name.
Now that I walk alone, there is not a regret,
so proud to have loved you, indeed, love you yet.

Curiously, around the time Margaret took sick, and
she was sick for about a year, Bob started writing poetry.
I say started, because for all his life no poetry had ever
been forthcoming, but now that the tap was opened,
it couldn't be turned off. Poem after poem came forth

and he soon had a book of over sixty poems published. This was only the beginning. By now he has written at least a thousand poems, and on it goes. As Bob says, the muse of poetry keeps blessing.

Thoughts that come and go from secret source,
to poets first appear, then run their course.
These mellow fellows lie at rest, supine,
seem careless, in their wanton waste of time.

Apparently, from labour choose to shirk.
Unfettered, though, these poets go to work.
Thoughts wild or mellow formulate in head,
of horizontal fellow on his bed.

Unbidden, raid, invade, unconsciousness.
Create, then formulate, for poetess.
Whence come they, what reservoir so deep,
through endless night as poets fight, to sleep.

Seek inaction, flee distraction, find repose.
Intercept the Muse of Poem, or Muse of Prose.
Poetic thought engages not, just out of hand,
imaginations agitation, inspires creation grand.

Are poets minds asleep, we cannot see,
or frenetically engaged creatively.
Surreal thought congeals hot, is caught, then dies.
Thoughts from aught contending, synthesize.

Feral thoughts intrude, from whence their source.
Not quiet, as they riot, through their course.
Wild thoughts, compelled to meld, becoming whole,
pervading heart, invading fertile soul.

Now my friends, as thought engages thought,
no preconception lends, 'bout how they ought,
to formulate, in some direction new,
designing rhyming pleasures, just for you.

Combining lines, poet reclines, upon his bed,
recording timing, chiming, through his head.
What fare, from where, no poet ever knows.
When Muse departs, sad poet starts, to doze.

And so our hero became ensconced in his little White Rock condo, able to heat and eat frozen dinners without having to cook. These were kindly provided by Veterans Affairs to veterans who live on disability pensions.

I'm sure you remember the earlier account of Bob's frozen lungs in his army trip up north. Sitting all day at his computer keyboard writing poetry and reminiscing over the goodness of God and missing his wife very much.

Foggy sodden seaside day,
don't have to leave, he's free to stay.
Warm and snug in his retreat,
snug's what he said, need he repeat.

Don't have to venture out the door,
do what he likes at eighty four.
Keeps busy doing this and that,
contented in his little flat.

Some would say he's sedentary, au contraire,
he is not very far removed from busy life,
just low-key since he lost his wife.

Chapter Twenty

BY THE BEGINNING OF 2010, BOB HAD STRUGGLED on alone for the few years since he'd lost Margaret and the passage of time dimmed the pain to the point where he started to come alive again to the sweeter aspects of the world around him.

He was pleasantly surprised to discover that the ladies were beginning to look attractive again, particularly a queenly English lady, Agnes Mary, who attended the midweek mini-church. Bob reluctantly recited one or two of his poems at these events—that is, if they really begged him—and he noticed that the queenly one seemed to enjoy his poetry.

Well, that last statement must be corrected. It was Bob who begged to read his poetry, not the members of the group.

He was starting to wish his life was not so empty.

How strange in life,
one would survive through all those years,
still be alive, outlive everybody who lived
with you, through all life's tears.

Those who loved and showered care
disappearing here and there,
can't find lover anywhere,
she left, no one to love.

Poor heart could slip and skip a beat,
life without wife so incomplete.

From all the years Bob's carrying,
he's showing wear and tear.
Though much too old for marrying,
there's mental shilly-shallying,
still feels the need to care.

Half the man he used to be,
his other half is gone.
A woman's love's fulfilling,
seems to make a man more willing
to sing in life, a happy song.

Romancing now takes too much pep,
interest waning, lost a step,

maybe two or three.
Spirit's willing, flesh is weak,
wouldn't know to hear him speak,
imagination's free.

Faith in God is wonderful, eternal life proclaim.
But arms of flesh, a loving wife give comfort,
while we're in this life,
with now and then a little strife,
but worth it, just the same.

One Sunday when he arrived at church, Bob decided to throw his heavy coat in the car trunk rather than take it into church. As he slammed the trunk lid down, he was shocked to remember that his car keys were in that coat pocket. Now what to do? After the service, he searched the lobby for someone who might know how to open the car without a key.

A tale of heavens blessing now poetically unfold.
This tale I know will fascinate your mind.
It started several years ago, in Surrey I am told,
when a lady prayed to heaven,
if God would be so kind.

This lady's name was Agnes Mary Martin, so it was,
and the prayer she prayed, you'll find hard to believe.
She asked if God would send a friend
to visit her because,

she now was lonely
and long past the time to grieve.

Now I'll share a little secret,
Agnes Mary wouldn't care,
every time she prays, God always seems to hear.
My mind sees a room in heaven, angels working there,
called prayer central,
where she comes through loud and clear.

I see an angel rushing, Agnes Mary's prayer in hand,
marked "urgent", he delivers it non-stop,
where God gives it top priority, first in all the land,
and then scans below to check the current crop.

The angel said, there is a guy, McCluskey is his name,
he just mopes around with poetry all day.
I could go down and zap him,
he wouldn't know I came.
God said "Okay, but tell him what to say."

Poor old Bob McCluskey
didn't realize he'd been found,
when he noticed Agnes Mary Wednesday night.
The angel sprinkled angel dust, and love joy all around,
and McCluskey's goose was cooked, without a fight.

They now noticed one another,
and were very starry eyed,

and it wasn't long, he took her out for lunch.
Soon the wedding bells were ringing,
she became a blushing bride,
they'll live happily ever after...that's my hunch.

Just at that moment, he noticed Agnes Mary, the queenly one, in the lobby. On impulse, he asked her if she could help him out by driving him down to his home in White Rock to pick up a spare set of car keys. Fortunately for Bob, she was merciful, and when they arrived he invited her in to see his paintings. However, she demurely but firmly declined and said she'd just wait out in the car.

They returned to the church and Bob felt that the least he could do to thank her was to invite her out for lunch.

After lunch, Bob saw her home and asked, "What'll we do next Sunday?"

The upshot of it was that they began to make Sunday lunch a regular thing and Bob gradually ingratiated himself into her confidence. Agnes Mary would not believe that the key-in-the-trunk situation had been was an accident; she just knew that Bob had designed this as a ploy to get to know her. (Bob says he'll never tell.)

Now and again during their first summer, Agnes Mary would drive down to White Rock. She loved the seaside ambience, and they would enjoy the day at the beach together.

Agnes Mary Martin, my delightful new ami,
in her little black conveyance paid a visit,
to my condo down in White Rock
on a Saturday in May,
by the ocean in the sunshine
where she and I could play,
while our attention on each other, we would rivet.

The sun was shining brightly
and the temperature was warm
as we toddled down the hillside to the strand.
Where the ocean lapped so gently
against the shores embrace,
and the children chased their parents
with a happy laughing face,
while we watched them from the park bench,
it was grand.

Then as the day was waning,
and the shadows growing long,
we each enjoyed an ice cream cone so sweet.
We drove back up to her car
and bid adieu to White Rock's throng,
ascending up the hillside as we sang a 50's song,
then waved goodbye as she departed from my street.

This lovely English lady was growing fonder of Bob
as the weeks and months flew by, and Bob was growing
in affection for her. You must remember that they were

not kids by any means, she at eighty five and he at eighty four, but nevertheless they found themselves increasingly drawn together. You may remember how as teenagers you loved to bill and coo quietly so that your parents wouldn't hear you. Well, for all their age and dignity, that was Bob and Agnes Mary, the only difference being her fear that her kids might hear them!

One Sunday evening, while they were sitting in her kitchen and enjoying a cup of tea, they had a conversation about a word the pastor had emphasized in his sermon: commitment. Suddenly, without premeditation on Bob's part and right out of the blue for Agnes Mary, Bob turned to her, looking her right in the eye, and asked, "Will you marry me"?

With the equanimity and poise that only an eighty-five-year old English lady could have, Agnes Mary paused for a moment, looked him right back in the eye, and said yes.

Bob could have sworn that he heard her add "I thought you'd never ask," but she denies it vehemently so Bob must have been mistaken. Bob claims that he was so deeply under her spell that he can hardly remember popping the question. Agnes Mary is quite emphatic, though, that he did.

Bob's destiny it seemed to lonely roam,
through life's declining journey on his own.
Deep heart-cry doomed to fall on empty ear,
no passionate response for him to hear.
But hark! sweet accent gently wafting by,
what lilting dulcet tones, dare he reply.
Be still my heart! Oh ancient trembling one,
you dare to reach for love, at setting sun.
Yes! Wonder of all wonders, can this be,
this radiant rapport twixt she and he.
Two hearts to blend, to never miss a beat,
becoming one in life, a love complete,
to be together till their end of time,
sweet Agnes Mary rapturously thine.
Journeying through life to now find rest,
at Agnes Mary's gentle loving breast.

Chapter Twenty-One

AND NOW TO PLAN A WEDDING TO BRING TOGETHER A gangly girl from Birmingham, England who grew into a stately beauty, with an athletically inept Canadian lad who joined the army but never fired a shot in anger. Who could have imagined way back in the 1920s that these two, so different and born so far apart, would ever even know each other? What a path Agnes Mary's life took, crossing the Atlantic with a babe in arms, meeting a nice policeman in Saskatoon who couldn't wait to marry her and with whom she ultimately had six children, sixteen grandchildren, and thirteen great-grandchildren. While Bob, who had brief stints first in the Canadian Air Force, then the Merchant Marine and finally Canadian Army, never stayed long enough in any of them to achieve a rank above Private. Bob's official contribution to the world's population was three children, seven grandchildren and five great-grandchildren. At last count, anyway.

Two very different people, having existed so far apart for a lifetime of eighty-five years, for different reasons found themselves perched on the western edge of Canada wondering what had happened. At that advanced age, what could they offer each other? How much time could they possibly have together after all the planning and confusion, not to mention expense, of organising a large church wedding?

Whose house would they live in? Whose dishes would they use? Whose bed would they sleep in? Worst of all, how would Bob remember all the names of the enormous tribe that Agnes Mary had mothered?

And how about the false teeth? How do you keep that a secret? How would they hide all their warts and imperfections? Who would help whom out of bed in the morning? What about snoring—did she snore; did he snore? Fortunately, that one resolved itself, for nobody snored, thank the Lord. When you realize that almost all couples start out young and grow their afflictions to-gether over many years, you can see the problem. They didn't have many years! What you see is what you gets.

But never mind, for they did have a very happy church wedding. Both families were fully represented and practically the whole church came. You can see how happy they were from the wedding pictures at the back of this book.

And so we see a very happy, contented couple of senior citizens now wedded and toddling off together down life's pathway into eternity. As Bob expressed it poetically,

When the stately Agnes Mary
like an ocean liner very
very regally, sedately
settled into Bobby's life,
without imposition slightest
and with touch the very lightest
she tied up to my berth,
before I knew it, was my wife.
Married to my ocean liner,
life could not have been sublimer
as she slowly moved about
without the slightest hint of speed.
Like the mighty Ocean Mary,
she would chart her course with very
very little to belittle, very little to impede.
With our future looking cheery,
resting oft to not be weary,
we both slowly stroll the strand
displaying Mary's English charm.
As we quaff the ocean air
we saunter on without a care,
often seen together talking
while we're walking arm in arm.
Now this begins another life

with Queen Mary as my wife,
together every day we join in prayer.
It's so nice to sit together
in the house in stormy weather,
what's the hurry,
we're not going anywhere.

Chapter Twenty-Two

WE HAVE KEPT THIS LAST CHAPTER AS A KIND OF postscript. It contains a revelation that is very special to Bob and Agnes Mary, and is purposefully intended to be a tribute to the wonderful love and direction of God to all men in general, but most specifically to His intercession in the lives of Bob and Agnes Mary.

What we have not shared up until now is a very remarkable example of how God will work in men's lives, unknown and unheralded over many years. It reveals also that God does not favour any man; He loves us all, rich or poor, saved or unsaved, man or woman.

This part of the story begins in the late 1970s with the new Christian Bob attending a church in Toronto on Broadview Avenue, Faith Temple, pastored by a great man of God, Winston Nunes. Doctor Winston Nunes was in his seventies then, at the end of a lifetime of evangelizing, church planting, and pastoring all over the world, but particularly in the Canadian and American Northwest. It was his habit in these later years to embark once a year on a programmed speaking tour of many of the churches in the Northwest with which he had been associated over his lifetime.

Over the course of his travels that year, Winston was scheduled to speak one Sunday at a particular church in Vancouver. As was his custom, he gave an altar call at the end of the service. Amongst those who responded was a middle aged English lady who was attending that church for the first time only because her granddaughter Vanessa had pleaded with her to come. She was dramatically and wonderfully born again and baptized in the Holy Spirit that Sunday and went on for the rest of her life to serve and honour God and see all of her family also born again.

All this occurred on Canada's west coast in 1978 to Agnes Mary, married to Fred and with a large and growing family. Just a few short years before this, but in the middle of Canada, Bob, married to Margaret and also with a growing family, was similarly born again under the ministry of Doctor Winston Nunes. Bob serving the pastor at his home church while he was out west preparing Bob's next wife.

Some twenty-five years later, God directed Bob and Agnes Mary, both now widowed, to the same church in Vancouver. There are a lot of cities, many more towns, and thousands of churches across Canada, so how could this be? Not only that, now that He had them both in the same church, He had to draw them together.

God programmed this whole love story to make their latter years better than their former years, all to the praise and glory of God. And they lived happily ever after... amen.

As we complete this sparse biography of Agnes Mary and Bob, the date is January 20, 2016, the date of Agnes Mary's ninety-second birthday and two days past Bob's ninety-first birthday on January 18, 2016. Unless they are raptured beforehand, the not-too-distant future should see their demise and departure from this earth's last days imbroglio with great thankfulness that both their houses have been saved.

Agnes and Bob's wedding

Agnes Mary Martin
and
Bob McCluskey

Look for other volumes from
poet Bob McCluskey's prolific pen:

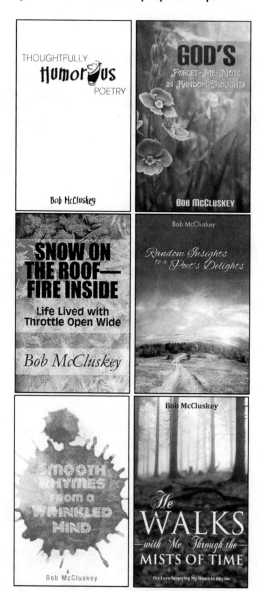